PREFACE
前 言

　　《电影中的英美文学名著》是基于编者多年从事英语文学名著相关课程教学经验而编写的，以英美广为人知的小说为主线，以培养学生了解英美文学大致脉络为宗旨，通过英美文学名著在电影与文本中展示的不同，激发学生对英美文学的兴趣。全书分为电影中的英国文学和美国文学两部分，共20章，每章包含背景、情节、电影版介绍、原文引用、电影片段推荐，以及讨论话题。每章需要2个以上课内学时和相当的课外学时。教师可以根据学生的具体情况对课时量进行适当调整。

　　本书的主要特点有以下几个方面：

　　1. 内容材料丰富。每章涉及一至两部名著，但也兼顾这一名著所处时期的文学大背景，给学生以有点有面的介绍，同时也鼓励学生课外阅读相关时期的文学知识，更全面地了解名著背景。

　　2. 电影版本和文字版本相结合。每篇文学名著都辅以一部根据原著改编的经典电影版本介绍，方便同学在课外时间观看，结合原著文本阅读，以进行批评性分析，更好地理解原著。

　　3. 每单元的讨论话题结合原著文本和电影版本，为学生提供不同角度的思考和讨论，提高学生对于文学原著的理解，并通过开放式的讨论，激发学生对文学原著的进一步阅读和研究。

　　《电影中的英美文学名著》由方凡和寿似琛老师合作编写。方凡老师的博士生高志香同学也协助进行了部分篇章的编写和校对工作。本书得到浙江大学本科生院的本科教材建设项目资助。在编写过程中，本书得到浙江大学外语学院多位老师的大力支持和协助，也得到浙江大学出版社张琛和李晨编辑的大力支持和协助，在此一并致谢。

　　不足或错讹之处敬请读者批评指正。

编　者

2018年8月15日于 浙大紫金港

CONTENTS

Part One 英国文学

Part Two　美国文学

Part One

英国文学

Chapter 1 *Beowulf*

Context

Composed by an unknown Anglo-Saxon poet around 700 A.D., *Beowulf* is often viewed both as the archetypal Anglo-Saxon literary work and as a cornerstone of modern literature. The plot of the poem concerns Scandinavian culture, recording the values and culture of a bygone era. Tiny tribes of people rally around strong kings, who protect their people from danger—especially from confrontations with other tribes. Strong kings demand bravery and loyalty from their warriors, whom they repay with treasures won in war. Mead-halls were places where warriors would gather in the presence of their lord to drink, boast, tell stories, and receive gifts, offering sanctuary. However, the early Middle Ages were a dangerous time, with the paranoid sense of foreboding and doom.

For the first hundred years of *Beowulf*'s prominence, interest in the poem was primarily historical. It was not until 1936, when the Oxford scholar J. R. R. Tolkien (who later wrote *The Hobbit* and *The Lord of the Rings*, works heavily influenced by *Beowulf*) published a groundbreaking paper entitled "Beowulf: The Monsters and the Critics" that the manuscript gained recognition as a serious work of art.

Beowulf was written in Old English. Compared to modern English, Old English is heavily Germanic, with little influence from Latin or French. Fortunately, most students encountering *Beowulf* read it in a form translated into modern English.

Plot

King Hrothgar of Denmark builds a great mead-hall, called Heorot, in which his warriors gather to drink, singing and laughing. Grendel, a horrible demon who lives in the swamplands of Hrothgar's kingdom, is angered by the noise, killing warriors one by one. A young Geatish warrior named Beowulf, inspired by the challenge, sails to Denmark with a small company of men, determined to defeat Grendel. Hrothgar accepts Beowulf's offer to fight Grendel and holds a feast for him, which lasts merrily into the night. Grendel arrives. Beowulf fights him unarmed, tearing the monster's arm off. The mortally wounded Grendel slinks back into the swamp to die. His mother comes to seek revenge for the son's death. Beowulf fights Grendel's mother and kills her. Beowulf's fame spreads across the kingdom. He returns to Geatland and ascends to the throne of the Geats with 50 years rule. When Beowulf is an old man, a dragon guarding a horde of treasures is enraged by a thief, unleashing fiery destruction on the Geats. With the help of a young warrior, Beowulf succeeds in killing the beast, but with a mortal wound in the neck. Beowulf dies and is buried in a place overlooking the sea.

＼ Suggested Movie Version

Beowulf (2007 film) is a 3D motion capture computer adult animated action adventure fantasy film directed by Robert Zemeckis and written by Neil Gaiman and Roger Avary. The title character, Beowulf, is portrayed by Ray Winstone and the antagonists Grendel and his mother are portrayed by Crispin Glover and Angelina Jolie respectively.

Author Neil Gaiman and screenwriter Roger Avary wrote a screen adaptation of *Beowulf* in May 1997. Some changes are made by the film. One objective of their adaptation was to offer their own interpretation for motivations behind Grendel's behavior and for what happened when Beowulf was in the cave of Grendel's mother. "It occurred to me that Grendel has always been described as the son of Cain, meaning half-man, half-demon, but his mother was always said to be full demon. So who's the father? It must be Hrothgar, and Grendel is dragging men back to the cave then it must be for the mother, so that she can attempt to sire another of demonkind."[1] said Roger Avary. The movie focuses much more on Grendel and his mother. While the dragon part is much less described.

＼ Important Quotations

Ⅹ Ⅹ The Mother of Grendel

They sank then to slumber. With sorrow one paid for

His evening repose, as often betid them

While Grendel was holding the gold-bedecked palace,

Ill-deeds performing, till his end overtook him,

Death for his sins. 'Twas seen very clearly,

Known unto earth-folk, that still an avenger

Outlived the loathed one, long since the sorrow

Caused by the struggle; the mother of Grendel,

Devil-shaped woman, her woe ever minded,

Who was held to inhabit the horrible waters,

The cold-flowing currents, after Cain had become a

Slayer-with-edges to his one only brother,

The son of his sire; he set out then banished,

Marked as a murderer, man-joys avoiding,

Lived in the desert. Thence demons unnumbered

---

[1] Tom Ambrose (December 2007). "He Is Legend". Empire. pp. 139–142.

Fate-sent awoke; one of them Grendel,

Sword-cursèd, hateful, who at Heorot met with

A man that was watching, waiting the struggle,

Where a horrid one held him with hand-grapple sturdy;

Nathless he minded the might of his body,

The glorious gift God had allowed him,

And folk-ruling Father's favor relied on,

His help and His comfort: so he conquered the foeman,

The hell-spirit humbled: he unhappy departed then,

Reaved of his joyance, journeying to death-haunts,

Foeman of man. His mother moreover

Eager and gloomy was anxious to go on

Her mournful mission, mindful of vengeance

For the death of her son. She came then to Heorot

Where the Armor-Dane earlmen all through the building

Were lying in slumber. Soon there became then

Return to the nobles, when the mother of Grendel

Entered the folk-hall; the fear was less grievous

By even so much as the vigor of maidens,

War-strength of women, by warrior is reckoned,

When well-carved weapon, worked with the hammer,

Blade very bloody, brave with its edges,

Strikes down the boar-sign that stands on the helmet.

Then the hard-edgèd weapon was heaved in the building,

The brand o'er the benches, broad-lindens many

Hand-fast were lifted; for helmet he recked not,

For armor-net broad, whom terror laid hold of.

She went then hastily, outward would get her

Her life for to save, when some one did spy her;

Soon she had grappled one of the athelings

Fast and firmly, when fenward she hied her;

That one to Hrothgar was liefest of heroes

In rank of retainer where waters encircle,

A mighty shield-warrior, whom she murdered at slumber,

A broadly-famed battle-knight. Beowulf was absent,

But another apartment was erstwhile devoted

To the glory-decked Geatman when gold was distributed.

There was hubbub in Heorot. The hand that was famous

She grasped in its gore; grief was renewed then

In homes and houses: 'twas no happy arrangement

In both of the quarters to barter and purchase

With lives of their friends. Then the well-agèd ruler,

The gray-headed war-thane, was woful in spirit,

When his long-trusted liegeman lifeless he knew of,

His dearest one gone. Quick from a room was

Beowulf brought, brave and triumphant.

As day was dawning in the dusk of the morning,

Went then that earlman, champion noble,

Came with comrades, where the clever one bided

Whether God all gracious would grant him a respite

After the woe he had suffered. The war-worthy hero

With a troop of retainers trod then the pavement

(The hall-building groaned), till he greeted the wise one,

The earl of the Ingwins; asked if the night had

Fully refreshed him, as fain he would have it.

ХХI Hrothgar's Account of the Monsters

Hrothgar rejoined, helm of the Scyldings:

"Ask not of joyance! Grief is renewed to

The folk of the Danemen. Dead is Æschere,

Yrmenlaf's brother, older than he,

My true-hearted counsellor, trusty adviser,

Shoulder-companion, when fighting in battle

Our heads we protected, when troopers were clashing,

And heroes were dashing; such an earl should be ever,

An erst-worthy atheling, as Æschere proved him.

The flickering death-spirit became in Heorot

His hand-to-hand murderer; I can not tell whither

The cruel one turned in the carcass exulting,

By cramming discovered. The quarrel she wreaked then,

That last night igone Grendel thou killedst

In grewsomest manner, with grim-holding clutches,

Since too long he had lessened my liege-troop and wasted

My folk-men so foully. He fell in the battle

With forfeit of life, and another has followed,

A mighty crime-worker, her kinsman avenging,

And henceforth hath 'stablished her hatred unyielding,

As it well may appear to many a liegeman,

Who mourneth in spirit the treasure-bestower,

Her heavy heart-sorrow; the hand is now lifeless

Which availed you in every wish that you cherished.

Land-people heard I, liegemen, this saying,

Dwellers in halls, they had seen very often

A pair of such mighty march-striding creatures,

Far-dwelling spirits, holding the moorlands:

One of them wore, as well they might notice,

The image of woman, the other one wretched

In guise of a man wandered in exile,

Except he was huger than any of earthmen;

Earth-dwelling people entitled him Grendel

In days of yore: they know not their father,

Whe'r ill-going spirits any were borne him

Ever before. They guard the wolf-coverts,

Lands inaccessible, wind-beaten nesses,

Fearfullest fen-deeps, where a flood from the mountains

'Neath mists of the nesses netherward rattles,

The stream under earth: not far is it henceward

Measured by mile-lengths that the mere-water standeth,

Which forests hang over, with frost-whiting covered,

A firm-rooted forest, the floods overshadow.

There ever at night one an ill-meaning portent

A fire-flood may see; 'mong children of men

None liveth so wise that wot of the bottom;

Though harassed by hounds the heath-stepper seek for,

Fly to the forest, firm-antlered he-deer,

Spurred from afar, his spirit he yieldeth,

His life on the shore, ere in he will venture

To cover his head. Uncanny the place is:

Thence upward ascendeth the surging of waters,

Wan to the welkin, when the wind is stirring

The weathers unpleasing, till the air groweth gloomy,

And the heavens lower. Now is help to be gotten

From thee and thee only! The abode thou know'st not,

The dangerous place where thou'rt able to meet with

The sin-laden hero: seek if thou darest!

For the feud I will fully fee thee with money,

With old-time treasure, as erstwhile I did thee,

With well-twisted jewels, if away thou shalt get thee."

Quoted from

http://www.gutenberg.org/files/16328/16328-h/16328-h.htm.

Clip of the Movie

The part when Beowulf and Grendel's mother meet each other.

Topics for Discussion

1. Does the image of Beowulf in the film meet your expectation of a hero in the Middle Age? Why or why not?

2. What's the purpose for the film director to choose Angelina Jolie to portray Grendel's mother? What role did women play in *Beowulf*?

3. In the original poem, the father of Grendel is neglected. In the film version, the father of Grendel seems to be the King Hrothgar. Can you accept it? Why or why not?

Chapter 2　Shakespeare: *Much Ado About Nothing*

＼ Context

William Shakespeare (1564—1616) was born in Stratford-upon-Avon, England. With not much formal education, Shakespeare eventually became the most popular playwright in England. He was also a favorite of Elizabeth I (ruled 1558—1603) and James I (ruled 1603—1625). His works, including 37 plays and 154 sonnets, were collected and printed which established his reputation in the early 18th century.

Much Ado About Nothing, probably written in 1598 and 1599, one of Shakespeare's best comedies, shows elements of happiness and also serious meditations on death, honor, shame, and also court politics. Often, Shakespeare treats death as part of the natural cycle of life. *Much Ado About Nothing* creates a very strong sense of anger, betrayal, hatred, grief, and despair. Many critics have noted that the plot of *Much Ado About Nothing* shares significant elements with that of *Romeo and Juliet*.

Besides the young lovers Hero and Claudio, there are older, wiser lovers Benedick and Beatrice. Benedick and Beatrice argue with delightful wit, and a rich sense of humor and compassion. Compared with other lovers in Shakespeare's comedies, Benedick and Beatrice are older and more mature, though they sometimes are childish when it comes to love.

＼ Plot

Leonato is a kindly nobleman who lives with his daughter Hero and his niece Beatrice in the Itlaian town of Messina. Prince Don Pedro just comes from a war with his two fellow soldiers: Claudio and Benedick, and his illegitimate brother Prince Don John, and they are invited to visit the town. Claudio falls in love with Hero. With the help of the Prince, the two young lovers are permitted to get married soon. While waiting for the coming wedding, Beatrice and Benedick are tricked by the Prince and his friends and fall in love. However, Don John makes Don Pedro and Claudio believe by evil tricks that Hero is not a faithful lady. With a fury, Claudio humiliates Hero on the wedding and abandons her. The stricken family decide to pretend that Hero is dead, expecting that Hero's innocence may come to light someday. At this critical moment, Benedick and Beatrice confess their love to each other. The truth happens to come out because the night watchmen overhears Don Jonh's followers' bragging about their crime accidentally. Leonato punishes Claudio to marry his "niece", who turns out to be Hero herself. Happily the two couples celebrate their wedding.

Suggested Movie Version

Much Ado About Nothing (1993) was adapted for the screen and directed by Kenneth Branagh, a Northern Irish actor, director and producer. Kenneth Branagh and his wife Emma Thompson also starred in the film as Benedick and Beatrice. The film became one of the most financially successful Shakespeare films ever released and entered into 1993 Cannes Film Festival.

The beautiful music to the film was composed by Kenneth Brahagh's collaborator Patrick Doyle, such as "Sigh No More Ladies", and "Pardon, Goddess of the Night". Emma Thompson won the Best Actress of Evening Standard British Film Awards and Kenneth Branagh won British Producer of the Year for London Film Critics' Circle.

Important Quotations

ACT IV Scene 1 A Church

Leonato. What shall become of this? what will this do?

Friar Francis. Marry, this well carried shall on her behalf

Change slander to remorse; that is some good.

But not for that dream I on this strange course,

But on this travail look for greater birth.

She dying, as it must so be maintain'd,

Upon the instant that she was accused,

Shall be lamented, pitied and excused

Of every hearer; for it so falls out

That what we have we prize not to the worth

Whiles we enjoy it, but being lack'd and lost,

Why, then we rack the value, then we find

The virtue that possession would not show us

Whiles it was ours. So will it fare with Claudio.

When he shall hear she died upon his words,

The idea of her life shall sweetly creep

Into his study of imagination,

And every lovely organ of her life

Shall come apparell'd in more precious habit,

More moving delicate, and, full of life,

Into the eye and prospect of his soul,

Than when she lived indeed; then shall he mourn,

(If ever love had interest in his liver)

And wish he had not so accused her—

No, though he thought his accusation true.

Let this be so, and doubt not but success

Will fashion the event in better shape

Than I can lay it down in likelihood.

But if all aim but this be levell'd false,

The supposition of the lady's death

Will quench the wonder of her infamy.

And if it sort not well, you may conceal her,

As best befits her wounded reputation,

In some reclusive and religious life,

Out of all eyes, tongues, minds and injuries.

Benedick. Signior Leonato, let the friar advise you;

And though you know my inwardness and love

Is very much unto the prince and Claudio,

Yet, by mine honour, I will deal in this

As secretly and justly as your soul

Should with your body.

Leonato. Being that I flow in grief,

The smallest twine may lead me.

Friar Francis. 'Tis well consented. presently away;

For to strange sores strangely they strain the cure.

Come, lady, die to live. This wedding day

Perhaps is but prolong'd. Have patience and endure.

[*Exeunt all but Benedick and Beatrice*]

Benedick. Lady Beatrice, have you wept all this while?

Beatrice. Yea, and I will weep a while longer.

Benedick. I will not desire that.

Beatrice. You have no reason; I do it freely.

Benedick. Surely I do believe your fair cousin is wronged.

Beatrice. Ah, how much might the man deserve of me that would right her!

Benedick. Is there any way to show such friendship?

Beatrice. A very even way, but no such friend.

Benedick. May a man do it?

Beatrice. It is a man's office, but not yours.

Benedick. I do love nothing in the world so well as you. Is not that strange?

Beatrice. As strange as the thing I know not. It were as possible for me to say I loved nothing so well as you. But believe me not; and yet I lie not. I confess nothing, nor I deny nothing. I am sorry for my cousin.

Benedick. By my sword, Beatrice, thou lovest me.

Beatrice. Do not swear, and eat it.

Benedick. I will swear by it that you love me; and I will make him eat it that says I love not you.

Beatrice. Will you not eat your word?

Benedick. With no sauce that can be devised to it. I protest I love thee.

Beatrice. Why, then, God forgive me!

Benedick. What offence, sweet Beatrice?

Beatrice. You have stayed me in a happy hour. I was about to protest I loved you.

Benedick. And do it with all thy heart.

Beatrice. I love you with so much of my heart that none is left to protest.

Benedick. Come, bid me do any thing for thee.

Beatrice. Kill Claudio.

Benedick. Ha! not for the wide world!

Beatrice. You kill me to deny it. Farewell.

Benedick. Tarry, sweet Beatrice.

Beatrice. I am gone, though I am here: there is no love in you. Nay, I pray you, let me go.

Benedick. Beatrice,—

Beatrice. In faith, I will go.

Benedick. We'll be friends first.

Beatrice. You dare easier be friends with me than fight with mine enemy.

Benedick. Is Claudio thine enemy?

Beatrice. Is he not approved in the height a villain, that hath slandered, scorned, dishonoured my kinswoman? O that I were a man! What, bear her in hand until they come to take hands; and then, with public accusation, uncovered slander, unmitigated rancour, —O God, that I were a man! I would eat his heart in the market place.

Benedick. Hear me, Beatrice!

Beatrice. Talk with a man out at a window! A proper saying!

Benedick. Nay, but, Beatrice—

Beatrice. Sweet Hero! She is wronged, she is slandered, she is undone.

Benedick. Beat—

Beatrice. Princes and counties! Surely, a princely testimony, a goodly count, Count Comfect, a sweet gallant surely! O that I were a man for his sake! or that I had any friend would be a man for my sake! But manhood is melted into courtesies, valour into compliment, and men are only turned into tongue, and trim ones too. He is now as valiant as Hercules that only tells a lie, and swears it. I cannot be a man with wishing, therefore I will die a woman with grieving.

Benedick. Tarry, good Beatrice. By this hand, I love thee.

Beatrice. Use it for my love some other way than swearing by it.

Benedick. Think you in your soul the Count Claudio hath wronged Hero?

Beatrice. Yea, as sure as I have a thought or a soul.

Benedick. Enough, I am engaged; I will challenge him. I will kiss your hand, and so I leave you. By this hand, Claudio shall render me a dear account. As you hear of me, so think of me. Go, comfort your cousin. I must say she is dead—and so, farewell.

Quoted from

http://www.opensourceshakespeare.org/views/plays/play_view.php?WorkID=mucha do&Act=4&Scene=1&Scope=scene

Clip of the Movie

The part of the wedding.

Topics for Discussion

1. Benedick and Beatrice are quarrelsome lovers. They are both feisty, cynical, witty and sharp and always trying to outwit, outsmart and outinsult the other. Do those two in the film version match your imagination of the two characters? Why or why not?

2. The music in the film is very beautiful. What's the role of music in this play and also in most of Shakespeare's plays?

3. What's the part of religion in this play? Friar Francis in the wedding witnesses the disruption of the wedding and offers suggestions for the wronged Hero. Do you agree with his suggestion?

Chapter 3　Defoe and Swift: *Robinson Crusoe* and *Gulliver's Travels*

Unit 1　Defoe: *Robinson Crusoe*

＼ Context

Daniel Defoe's protestant values endured throughout his life despite discrimination and persecution, and these values are expressed in *Robinson Crusoe*. In 1683, Defoe visited Holland, France, and Spain on business, and he developed a taste for travel that lasted throughout his life. His characters Moll Flanders and Robinson Crusoe both change their lives by voyaging far from their native England. Defoe worked as a publicist, political journalist, and pamphleteer for Harley and other politicians. He also worked as a spy, reveling in aliases and disguises, reflecting his own variable identity as merchant, poet, journalist, and prisoner. This theme of changeable identity would later be expressed in the life of Robinson Crusoe, who becomes merchant, slave, plantation owner, and even unofficial king. In his writing, Defoe often used a pseudonym simply because he enjoyed the effect.

Defoe began writing fiction late in life, around the age of sixty. He published his first novel, *Robinson Crusoe,* in 1719, attracting a large middle-class readership. The focus on the actual conditions of everyday life and avoidance of the courtly and the heroic made Defoe a revolutionary in English literature and helped define the new genre of the novel. Stylistically, Defoe was a great innovator. Dispensing with the ornate style associated with the upper classes, Defoe used the simple, direct, fact-based style of the middle classes, which became the new standard for the English novel. With *Robinson Crusoe*'s theme of solitary human existence, Defoe paved the way for the central modern theme of alienation and isolation.

＼ Plot

After surviving a storm, Robinson Crusoe and the others are shipwrecked. He is thrown upon shore only to discover that he is the sole survivor of the wreck. Crusoe makes immediate plans for food, and then shelter, to protect himself from wild animals. He brings as many things as possible from the wrecked ship, things that would be useful later to him. In addition, he begins to develop talents that he has never used in order to provide himself with necessities. Cut off from the company of men, he begins to communicate with God, thus beginning the first part of his religious conversion. To keep his sanity and to entertain himself, he begins a journal. In the journal, he records every task that he performs each day since he has been marooned. As time passes, Crusoe became a skilled craftsman, able to construct many useful things, and thus furnishes himself with diverse comforts. He also learns about farming, as a result of some seeds which he brings with him. An illness prompts some prophetic dreams, and Crusoe begins to reappraise his duty to God. Crusoe explores his island and discoveres another part of the island much richer and more fertile, and he builds a summer home there. One of the first tasks he undertook is to build himself a canoe in case an escape becomes possible, but the canoe is too heavy to get to the water. He then constructs a small boat and journeys around the island. After spending about fifteen years on the island, Crusoe finds a man's naked footprint. Sometime later, Crusoe is horrified to find human bones scattered about the shore, evidently the remains of a savage feast. Crusoe is cautious for several years, but encounters nothing more to alarm him. He finds a cave, which he uses as a storage room, and in December of the same year, he spies cannibals sitting around a campfire. He does not see them again for quite some time. Later, Crusoe saw a ship in distress, but everyone is already drowned on the ship and Crusoe remains companionless. However, he is able to take many provisions from this newly wrecked ship. Sometime later, cannibals land on the island and a victim escapes. Crusoe saves his life, names him Friday, and teaches him English. Friday soon becomes Crusoe's humble and devoted slave. Crusoe and Friday make plans to leave the island. They save two prisoners from the cannibals since one is a white man. The white man is a Spaniard and the other is Friday's father. A week later, they spy a ship but they quickly learn that there has been a mutiny on board. Crusoe and Friday rescue the captain and two other men, and after much scheming, regain control of the ship. The grateful captain gives Crusoe many gifts and takes him and Friday back to England. Crusoe returns to England and finds that in his absence he has become a wealthy man. After going to Lisbon to handle some of his affairs, Crusoe begins an overland journey back to England. Crusoe and his company encounter many hardships in crossing the mountains, but they finally arrive safely in England. Crusoe sells his plantation in Brazil for a good price, marries, and has three children. Finally, however, he is persuaded to go on yet another voyage, and he visits his old island, where there are promises of new adventures to be found in a later account.

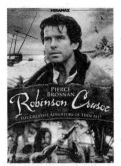

❧ Suggested Movie Version

Robinson Crusoe is a 1997 Australian-American action adventure film based on Daniel Defoe's classic novel. Although titled "Daniel Defoe's *Robinson Crusoe*" in various releases, the film differs markedly from the original book.

The film opens to a fictionalized Daniel Defoe being offered to read a castaway's autobiography. He grudgingly obliges and begins to get engrossed in the narrative. In the film, Crusoe is portrayed as being a Scotsman with a love interest. The title of the novel states that its main character is from York, in Northern England. In the film Crusoe flees by sea to escape being hunted down by the family of the friend he killed. In the novel, Crusoe departs against his parents' wishes, due to a longing for adventure. In the film he initially spends less than a year at sea before being shipwrecked. Crusoe in the book is stranded on multiple occasions and at sea much longer; he spends time on numerous ships in a variety of places. In the film his ship founders near New Guinea in the vicinity of New Britain. The island in the novel is near Venezuela off the mouth of the Orinoco River.

Crusoe's interactions with people—particularly Friday—vary considerably. In the film Crusoe comes to accept Friday's culture. This is the opposite of the theology of the novel, where Friday converts to Christianity. The film also avoids all instances of mutineers and European prisoners that lead to Crusoe's rescue in the original novel.

Crusoe's rescue in the book occurs when he helps the captain of a mutinous vessel in return for a passage home. The mutineers are left on the island instead. In the film, Crusoe is wounded by Friday's enemies and Friday takes him to his own island to be healed, but Friday's tribe has disowned him, and force Crusoe and Friday to fight to the death after saying they will allow the winner to go free. Just as Friday is about to kill Crusoe, a slaver ship arrives and kills Friday before enslaving his tribe and razing their village. Crusoe then returns to Scotland. In the novel, Friday is not killed and accompanies Crusoe on his return to England, where he begins another round of adventures.

╲ Important Quotations

Chapter 1

I was born in the year 1632, in the city of York, of a good family, though not of that country, my father being a foreigner of Bremen, who settled first at Hull. He got a good estate by merchandise, and leaving off his trade lived afterward at York, from whence he had married my mother, whose relations were named Robinson, a good family in that country, and from whom I was called Robinson Kreutznear; but by the usual corruption of words in England we are now called, nay, we call ourselves, and write our name, Crusoe, and so my companions always called me.

I had two elder brothers, one of which was lieutenant-colonel to an English regiment of foot in Flanders, formerly commanded by the famous Colonel Lockhart, and was killed at the battle near Dunkirk against the Spaniards; what became of my second brother I never knew, any more than my father and mother did know what was become of me.

Being the third son of the family, and not bred to any trade, my head began to be filled very early with rambling thoughts. My father, who was very ancient, had given me a competent share of learning, as far as house-education and a country free school generally goes, and designed me for the law, but I would be satisfied with nothing but going to sea; and my inclination to this led me so strongly against the will, nay, the commands, of my father, and against all the entreaties and persuasions of my mother and other friends, that there seemed to be something fatal in that propension of nature tending directly to the life of misery which was to befall me.

Chapter 16

My island was now peopled, and I thought myself very rich in subjects; and it was a merry reflection, which I frequently made, how like a king I looked. First of all, the whole country was my own mere property, so that I had an undoubted right of dominion. Secondly, my people were perfectly subjected. I was absolute lord and lawgiver; they all owned their lives to me, and were ready to lay down their lives, if there had been occasion of it, for me. It was remarkable, too, we had but three subjects, and they were of three different religions. My man Friday was a Protestant, his father was a pagan and a cannibal, and the Spaniard was a papist. However, I allowed liberty of conscience throughout my dominions. But this is by the way.

As soon as I had secured my two weak rescued prisoners, and given them shelter and a place to rest them upon, I began to think of making some provision for them; and the first thing I did, I ordered Friday to take a yearling goat, betwixt a kid and a goat, out of my particular flock, to be killed; when I cut off the hinder-quarter, and chopping it into small pieces. I set Friday to work to boiling and stewing, and made them a very good dish, I assure you, of flesh and broth, having put some barley and rice also into the broth; and as I cooked it without doors, for I made no fire within my inner wall, so I carried it all into the new tent, and having set a table there for them, I sat down and ate my own dinner also with them, and as well as I could cheered them, and encouraged them; Friday being my interpreter, especially to his father, and, indeed, to the Spaniard too; for the Spaniard spoke the language of the savages pretty well.

After we had dined, or rather supped, I ordered Friday to take one of the canoes and go and fetch our muskets and other fire-arms, which, for want of time, we had left upon the place of battle; and the next day I ordered him to go and bury the dead bodies of the savages, which lay open to the sun, and would presently be offensive; and I also ordered him to bury the horrid remains of their barbarous feast, which I knew were pretty much, and which I could not think of doing myself; nay, I could not bear to see them, if I went that way. All which he punctually performed, and defaced the very appearance of the savages being there; so that when I went again I could scarce know where it was, otherwise than by the corner of the wood pointing to the place.

I then began to enter into a little conversation with my two new subjects; and first, I set Friday to inquire of his father what he thought of the escape of the savages in that canoe, and whether we might expect a return of them, with a power too great for us to resist. His first opinion was, that the savages in the boat never could live out the storm which blew that night they went off, but must, of necessity, be drowned, or driven south to those other shores, where they were as sure to be devoured as they were to be drowned if they were cast away. But as to what they would do if they came safe on shore, he said he knew not; but it was his opinion that they were so dreadfully frightened with the manner of their being attacked, the noise, and the fire, that he believed they would tell their people they were all killed by thunder and lightning, not by the hand of man; and that the two which appeared, viz., Friday and me, were two heavenly spirits, or furies, come down to destroy them, and not men with weapons. This, he said, he knew, because he heard them all cry out so in their language to one another; for it was impossible to them to conceive that a man could dart fire, and speak thunder, and kill at a distance without lifting up the hand, as was done now. And this old savage was in the right; for, as I understood since by other hands, the savages never attempted to go over to the island afterwards. They were so terrified with the accounts given by those four men (for, it seems, they did escape the sea) that they believed whoever went to that enchanted island would be destroyed with fire from the gods.

Quoted from

http://ishare.iask.sina.com.cn/f/5611507.html.

Clip of the Movie

The part when Crusoe and Friday had to fight against each other in order to be set free, and finally Friday was killed by a slaver ship when he was about to kill Crusoe.

Topics for Discussion

1. What do you think of Crusoe's acceptance of Friday's culture instead of Friday's being converted to Christianity in the movie?

2. What do you think of the pace and rhythm of the film compared with the novel? Does it show sufficient information for the audience to have a better and deeper understanding of the movie?

Unit2   Swift: *Gulliver's Travels*

✎ Context

During Jonathan Swift's brief time in England, Swift had become friends with writers such as Alexander Pope, and they decided to write satires of modern learning. The third voyage of *Gulliver's Travels* is assembled from the work Swift did during this time. However, the final work was not completed until 1726, and the narrative of the third voyage was actually the last one completed. *Gulliver's Travels* was a controversial work when it was first published in 1726. In fact, it was not until almost ten years after its first printing that the book appeared with the entire text that Swift had originally intended it to have. Ever since, editors have excised many of the passages, particularly the more caustic ones dealing with bodily functions. Even without those passages, however, *Gulliver's Travels* serves as a biting satire, and Swift ensures that it is both humorous and critical, constantly attacking British and European society through its descriptions of imaginary countries. *Gulliver's Travels* is about a specific set of political conflicts, but if it were nothing more than that it would long ago have been forgotten. The staying power of the work comes from its depiction of the human condition and its often despairing, but occasionally hopeful, sketch of the possibilities for humanity to rein in its baser instincts.

ꤾ Plot

Gulliver's Travels recounts the story of Lemuel Gulliver, a practical-minded Englishman trained as a surgeon who takes to the seas when his business fails. In a deadpan first-person narrative that rarely shows any signs of self-reflection or deep emotional response, Gulliver narrates the adventures that befall him on these travels. Gulliver's adventure in Lilliput begins when he wakes after his shipwreck to find himself bound by innumerable tiny threads and addressed by tiny captors who are in awe of him but fiercely protective of their kingdom. They are not afraid to use violence against Gulliver, though their arrows are little more than pinpricks. But overall, they are hospitable, risking famine in their land by feeding Gulliver, who consumes more food than a thousand Lilliputians combined could. Eventually Gulliver becomes a national resource, used by the army in its war against the people of Blefuscu. But things change when Gulliver is convicted of treason for putting out a fire in the royal palace with his urine and is condemned to be shot in the eyes and starved to death. Gulliver escapes to Blefuscu, where he is able to repair a boat he finds and set sail for England.

After staying in England with his wife and family for two months, Gulliver undertakes his next sea voyage, which takes him to a land of giants called Brobdingnag. Here, a field worker discovers him. The farmer initially treats him as little more than an animal, keeping him for amusement. The farmer eventually sells Gulliver to the queen, who makes him a courtly diversion and is entertained by his musical talents. He is generally startled by the ignorance of the people here—even the king knows nothing about politics. Gulliver leaves Brobdingnag when his cage is plucked up by an eagle and dropped into the sea.

Next, Gulliver sets sail again and, after an attack by pirates, ends up in Laputa, where a floating island inhabited by theoreticians and academics oppresses the land below, called Balnibarbi. Gulliver is able to witness the conjuring up of figures from history, such as Julius Caesar and other military leaders.

Finally, on his fourth journey, Gulliver sets out as captain of a ship, but after the mutiny of his crew and a long confinement in his cabin, he arrives in an unknown land. This land is populated by

Houyhnhnms, rational-thinking horses who rule, and by Yahoos, brutish humanlike creatures who serve the Houyhnhnms. He is treated with great courtesy and kindness by the horses and is enlightened by his many conversations with them and by his exposure to their noble culture. He wants to stay with the Houyhnhnms, but his bared body reveals to the horses that he is very much like a Yahoo, and he is banished. Gulliver then concludes his narrative with a claim that the lands he has visited belong by rights to England, as her colonies, even though he questions the whole idea of colonialism.

﹨ Suggested Movie Version

Gulliver's Travels is a 1939 American cel-animated Technicolor feature film, about an explorer who helps a small kingdom who declared war after an argument over a wedding song. The film was released on December 22, 1939 by Paramount Pictures, who had the feature produced as an answer to the success of Walt Disney's box-office hit *Snow White and the Seven Dwarfs*. This is Paramount's first feature-length animated film.

Gulliver was the second cel-animated feature film ever released, and the first produced by an American studio other than Walt Disney Productions. The story is based very loosely upon the Lilliputian adventures of Gulliver depicted in Jonathan Swift's 18th century novel *Gulliver's Travels*.

﹨ Important Quotations

Part I   Chapter I

My father had a small estate in Nottinghamshire; I was the third of five sons. He sent me to Emanuel College in Cambridge at fourteen years old, where I resided three years, and applied myself close to my studies; but the charge of maintaining me, although I had a very scanty allowance, being too great for a narrow fortune, I was bound apprentice to Mr. James Bates, an eminent surgeon in London, with whom I continued four years. My father now and then sending me small sums of money, I laid them out in learning navigation, and other parts of the mathematics, useful to those who intend to travel, as I always believed it would be, some time or other, my fortune to do. When I left Mr. Bates, I went down to my father, where, by the assistance of him, and my uncle John and some other relations, I got forty pounds, and a promise of thirty pounds a year, to maintain me at Leyden. There I studied physic two years and seven months, knowing it would be useful in long voyages.

Soon after my return from Leyden, I was recommended by my good master, Mr. Bates, to be surgeon to the "Swallow", Captain Abraham Pannel, commander; with whom I continued three years and a half, making a voyage or two into the Levant, and some other parts. When I came back

I resolved to settle in London; to which Mr. Bates, my master, encouraged me, and by him I was recommended to several patients. I took part of a small house in the Old Jewry; and being advised to alter my condition, I married Mrs. Mary Burton, second daughter to Mr. Edmund Burton, hosier in Newgate-street, with whom I received four hundred pounds for a portion.

But my good master, Bates, dying in two years after, and I having few friends, my business began to fail; for my conscience would not suffer me to imitate the bad practice of too many among my brethren. Having, therefore, consulted with my wife, and some of my acquaintance, I determined to go again to sea. I was surgeon successively in two ships, and made several voyages, for six years, to the East and West Indies, by which I got some addition to my fortune. My hours of leisure I spent in reading the best authors, ancient and modern, being always provided with a good number of books; and when I was ashore, in observing the manners and dispositions of the people, as well as learning their language; wherein I had a great facility, by the strength of my memory.

The last of these voyages not proving very fortunate, I grew weary of the sea, and intended to stay at home with my wife and family. I removed from the Old Jewry to Fetter Lane, and from thence to Wapping, hoping to get business among the sailors; but it would not turn to account. After three years expectation that things would mend, I accepted an advantageous offer from Captain William Prichard, master of the "Antelope", who was making a voyage to the South Sea. We set sail from Bristol, May 4, 1699; and our voyage was at first very prosperous.

Part II   Chapter VI

Above all, he was amazed to hear me talk of a mercenary standing army, in the midst of peace, and among a free people. He said, "if we were governed by our own consent, in the persons of our representatives, he could not imagine of whom we were afraid, or against whom we were to fight; and would hear my opinion, whether a private man's house might not be better defended by himself, his children, and family, than by half-a-dozen rascals, picked up at a venture in the streets for small wages, who might get a hundred times more by cutting their throats?"

He laughed at my "odd kind of arithmetic," as he was pleased to call it, "in reckoning the numbers of our people, by a computation drawn from the several sects among us, in religion and politics." He said, "he knew no reason why those, who entertain opinions prejudicial to the public, should be obliged to change, or should not be obliged to conceal them. And as it was tyranny in any government to require the first, so it was weakness not to enforce the second: for a man may be allowed to keep poisons in his closet, but not to vend them about for cordials."

He observed, "that among the diversions of our nobility and gentry, I had mentioned gaming: he desired to know at what age this entertainment was usually taken up, and when it was laid down; how much of their time it employed; whether it ever went so high as to affect their fortunes; whether mean, vicious people, by their dexterity in that art, might not arrive at great riches, and sometimes keep our very nobles in dependence, as well as habituate them to vile companions, wholly take them from the improvement of their minds, and force them, by the losses they received, to learn and practise that infamous dexterity upon others?"

He was perfectly astonished with the historical account gave him of our affairs during the last century; protesting "it was only a heap of conspiracies, rebellions, murders, massacres, revolutions, banishments, the very worst effects that avarice, faction, hypocrisy, perfidiousness, cruelty, rage, madness, hatred, envy, lust, malice, and ambition, could produce."

His majesty, in another audience, was at the pains to recapitulate the sum of all I had spoken; compared the questions he made with the answers I had given; then taking me into his hands, and stroking me gently, delivered himself in these words, which I shall never forget, nor the manner he spoke them in: "My little friend Grildrig, you have made a most admirable panegyric upon your country; you have clearly proved, that ignorance, idleness, and vice, are the proper ingredients for qualifying a legislator; that laws are best explained, interpreted, and applied, by those whose interest and abilities lie in perverting, confounding, and eluding them. I observe among you some lines of an institution, which, in its original, might have been tolerable, but these half erased, and the rest wholly blurred and blotted by corruptions. It does not appear, from all you have said, how any one perfection is required toward the procurement of any one station among you; much less, that men are ennobled on account of their virtue; that priests are advanced for their piety or learning; soldiers, for their conduct or valour; judges, for their integrity; senators, for the love of their country; or counsellors for their wisdom. As for yourself," continued the king, "who have spent the greatest part of your life in travelling, I am well disposed to hope you may hitherto have escaped many vices of your country. But by what I have gathered from your own relation, and the answers I have with much pains wrung and extorted from you, I cannot but conclude the bulk of your natives to be the most pernicious race of little odious vermin that nature ever suffered to crawl upon the surface of the earth."

Part IV   Chapter XII

Having thus answered the only objection that can ever be raised against me as a traveller, I here take a final leave of all my courteous readers, and return to enjoy my own speculations in my little garden at Redriff; to apply those excellent lessons of virtue which I learned among the Houyhnhnms; to instruct the Yahoos of my own family, is far as I shall find them docible animals; to behold my figure often in a glass, and thus, if possible, habituate myself by time to tolerate the sight of a human creature; to lament the brutality to Houyhnhnms in my own country, but always treat their persons with respect, for the sake of my noble master, his family, his friends, and the whole Houyhnhnm race, whom these of ours have the honour to resemble in all their lineaments, however their intellectuals came to degenerate.

I began last week to permit my wife to sit at dinner with me, at the farthest end of a long table; and to answer (but with the utmost brevity) the few questions I asked her. Yet, the smell of a Yahoo continuing very offensive, I always keep my nose well stopped with rue, lavender, or tobacco leaves. And, although it be hard for a man late in life to remove old habits, I am not altogether out of hopes, in some time, to suffer a neighbour Yahoo in my company, without the apprehensions I am yet under of his teeth or his claws.

My reconcilement to the Yahoo kind in general might not be so difficult, if they would be content with those vices and follies only which nature has entitled them to. I am not in the least provoked at the sight of a lawyer, a pickpocket, a colonel, a fool, a lord, a gamester, a politician, a whoremonger, a physician, an evidence, a suborner, an attorney, a traitor, or the like; this is all according to the due course of things: but when I behold a lump of deformity and diseases, both in body and mind, smitten with pride, it immediately breaks all the measures of my patience; neither shall I be ever able to comprehend how such an animal, and such a vice, could tally together. The wise and virtuous Houyhnhnms, who abound in all excellences that can adorn a rational creature, have no name for this vice in their language, which has no terms to express any thing that is evil, except those whereby they describe the detestable qualities of their Yahoos, among which they were not able to distinguish this of pride, for want of thoroughly understanding human nature, as it shows itself in other countries where that animal presides. But I, who had more experience, could plainly observe some rudiments of it among the wild Yahoos.

But the Houyhnhnms, who live under the government of reason, are no more proud of the good qualities they possess, than I should be for not wanting a leg or an arm; which no man in his wits would boast of, although he must be miserable without them. I dwell the longer upon this subject from the desire I have to make the society of an English Yahoo by any means not insupportable; and therefore I here entreat those who have any tincture of this absurd vice, that they will not presume to come in my sight.

Quoted from
http://novel.tingroom.com/jingdian/823/.

Clip of the Movie
The part when Gulliver criticized the kings for starting the war at the end of the movie.

Topics for discussion

1. In his satire, Swift makes a correlation between size and morality. Explain how this works in the Travels, paying particular attention to Gulliver in Lilliput and in Brobdingnag.

2. Is the animated movie a better choice to represent the original novel? Is it more like a fairy tale and trying to avoid presenting some political problems with the impact of the success of *Snow White and the Seven Dwarfs* made by the same team?

3. What do you think of the differences between Defoe and Swift?

Chapter 4　Austen and Dickens: *Emma* and *Great Expectations*

Unit 1　Jane Austen: *Emma*

✎ Context

While *Pride and Prejudice* is doubtlessly Jane Austen's most widely read and popular novel, many critics aver that her fullest achievement, the masterpiece of her six completed novels, is *Emma*. At the time of its writing (January 21, 1814 to March 29, 1815) Miss Austen had reached a calm high point in her development as an artist, a point of steady, relaxed control over both her subject matter and her technique. The temporal substance of her novels—the manners and interests of the upper middle class in late eighteenth-and early nineteenth-century England—was that of her own surroundings from the beginning. Born on December 16, 1775, the seventh of eight children—six boys and two girls—she had more than common varied contact with the limited world of provincial gentry because her father was a country clergyman. Though she accompanied her elder sister Cassandra to two boarding schools only to return home at the age of nine to remain there, she had the advantage of growing up and studying in an educated family. In addition, the Austens were a novel-reading family. Before 1801, while Jane was still in her early twenties, she had written three unpublished novels: *Pride and Prejudice*, *Sense and Sensibility*, and *Northanger Abbey*. Upon removal to Chawton Cottage she began immediately to write again and, before her death on July 18, 1817, she completed, in order, *Mansfield Park*, *Emma*, and *Persuasion*. Beginning with the printing of *Sense and Sensibility* in 1811, each of the six novels was published, the new ones in short order after their completion, some of the works going into second and third, as well as French, editions by the time of her death. Jane Austen loved the life around her. But she also saw it clearly enough to perceive its imperfections along with its perfections: an insight into the divided nature of things that was to set its imprint of cool liveliness upon every page that she wrote. She was aware, of course, of worldly happenings: the distant thunder of the American and French revolutions, the rise of Napoleon, the industrial revolution, the British maritime mutinies, the overdone peculiarities of Gothic and sentimental novels, the new emotional quality of Romanticism. But most of these historic fluxes did not come even as close as the blank margin of her pages. Instead, she concentrated upon eternal mixed qualities of humanity—of human relationships—exemplified in the provincial society about her. This life she knew intimately, and it was for her enough.

Plot

Youthful Emma Woodhouse, whose long-time governess and friend Miss Taylor has just married Mr. Weston, takes some solace in being left alone with her aging father by claiming that she made the match herself. An old friend of the family, Mr. George Knightley, does not believe her, but in her certainty she decides that she must also marry off the young rector, Mr. Elton. Among her friends and acquaintances in the large and populous village of Highbury, she begins to notice young Harriet Smith. Determining first to improve Harriet, Emma discourages her interest in worthy Robert Martin of Abbey Mill Farm, declares that Harriet must be from more genteel parents than his, and fixes upon Harriet as Mr. Elton's future wife. Later, Emma finds herself alone with Mr. Elton in the second carriage. But she is disconcerted even more when he begins insistently to declare his love for her and when he is amazed to learn that she thought him in love with Harriet. It is Emma's unhappy duty to inform Harriet about Mr. Elton and to console her, inwardly blaming herself for being in error.

Miss Bates' orphan niece Jane Fairfax will arrive next week for a two-month visit. Jane, upon arrival, is elegant, accomplished, and reserved, and Emma does not like her when she learns that Jane and Frank Churchill have met at Weymouth. Frank Churchill finally arrives and is very agreeable and lively. From the time of his first visit to the Woodhouses, it is evident that Mr. and Mrs. Weston would like to make a match between him and Emma. Frank visits the Bateses and then the Woodhouses, leaving Emma pretty well convinced that he is in love with her, though she can picture herself only as refusing him. Mr. Knightley shows such respect for Jane Fairfax that Emma thinks he may be falling in love, but he declares that he would never ask her to marry him.

By the time Frank Churchill returns, Emma realizes that there is no attachment on her part. Harriet indicates that she is interested in someone above her, and Emma is sure that it is Frank. During a gathering at which they play a word game, Frank shoves words at Jane which make George Knightley suspect that the two are involved. Later she learns that Jane has accepted a position as governess and will be leaving soon. Frank too has to leave, but immediately, for Mrs. Churchill is ill and, in fact, soon dies. Emma feels sorry for Jane's having to take a position, but her attentions are repulsed. Ten days later the Westons receive a brief letter from Frank in which he explains that he and Jane have been engaged since their being together at Weymouth; Mr. Churchill now gives his consent. It turns out that Harriet has not been thinking of Frank at all but rather of George Knightley. When Emma learns this, she is awakened to the fact that Mr. Knightley must marry no one but herself and she wishes that she had never seen Harriet and had let her marry Robert Martin. Knightley returns from a business trip, learns the news, and commiserates with Emma, who assures him that she has never been captivated by Frank. The revelation leads Knightley to declare his own feelings for Emma, and they become engaged, though Emma knows that they cannot marry as long as she has to take care of her father, for she cannot leave him and he will not leave his home. A very reasonable letter from Frank to Mrs. Weston explains satisfactorily his conduct at Highbury and his and Jane's need for secrecy. Emma is relieved, but she cannot set her mind at rest about Harriet, who now goes to visit the John Knightleys in London. Emma and Jane become reconciled as friends; George Knightley decides that, since Emma cannot leave her father, he will live with them; then it takes the combined persuasive forces of Emma, Knightley, and the Westons to get Mr. Woodhouse to agree to the marriage. When Harriet decides to marry Robert Martin after all, Emma feels free enough that, after some small delaying tactics by Mr. Woodhouse, she and George Knightley are wed in "perfect happiness".

＼ Suggested Movie Version

Emma is a 1996 period film based on the novel of the same name by Jane Austen. Although in general staying close to the plot of the book, the screenplay by Douglas McGrath enlivens the banter between the staid Mr. Knightley and the vivacious Emma, making the basis of their attraction more apparent.

Austen's original novel deals with Emma's false sense of class superiority, for which she is eventually chastised. In an essay from *Jane Austen in Hollywood*, Nora Nachumi writes that, due partly to Paltrow's star status, Emma appears less humbled by the end of this film than she does in the novel.

While the movie trailer shows Emma in love with John and Frank, "Emma loves John" and "Emma loves Frank" are both displayed over film from the movie. Mr. Knightley's given name is George. It is George Knightley's brother who is named John, making this an error in the trailer.

The film has received generally positive reviews from critics. Ken Eisner, writing for *Variety*, proclaimed, "Gwyneth Paltrow shines brightly as Jane Austen's most endearing character, the disastrously self-assured matchmaker Emma Woodhouse. A fine cast, speedy pacing and playful direction make this a solid contender for the Austen sweepstakes."

＼ Important Quotations

Chatper 1

Mr. Knightley, in fact, was one of the few people who could see faults in Emma Woodhouse, and the only one who ever told her of them; and though this was not particularly agreeable to Emma herself, she knew it would be so much less so to her father, that she would not have him really suspect such a circumstance as her not being thought perfect by everybody. "Emma knows I never flatter her," said Mr. Knightley, "but I meant no reflection on anybody. Miss Taylor has been used to have two persons to please; she will now have but one. The chances are that she must be a gainer." "Well," said Emma, willing to let it pass, "you want to hear about the wedding; and I shall be happy to tell you, for we all behaved charmingly. Everybody was punctual, everybody in their best looks: not a tear, and hardly a long face to be seen. Oh, no; we all felt that we were going to be only half a mile apart, and were sure of meeting every day." "Dear Emma bears everything so well," said her father. "But, Mr. Knightley, she is really very sorry to lose poor Miss Taylor, and I am sure she will miss her more than she thinks for." Emma turned away her head, divided between tears and smiles. "It is impossible that Emma should not miss such a companion," said Mr. Knightley. "We should not like her so well as we do, sir, if we could suppose it: but she knows how much the marriage is to Miss Taylor's advantage; she knows how very acceptable it must be, at Miss Taylor's time of life, to be settled in a home of her own, and how important to her to be secure of a comfortable provision, and therefore cannot allow herself to feel so much pain as pleasure. Every friend of Miss Taylor must be glad to have her so happily married." "And you have forgotten one matter of joy to me," said Emma, "and a very considerable one—that I made the match myself. I made the match, you know, four years ago; and to have it take place, and be proved in the right, when so many people said Mr. Weston would never marry again, may comfort me for anything." Mr. Knightley shook his head at her. Her father fondly replied, "Ah! my dear, I wish you would not make matches and foretell things, for whatever you say always comes to pass. Pray do not make any more matches." "I Promise you to make none for myself, papa; but I must, indeed, for other people. It is the greatest amusement in the world! And after such success, you know! Everybody said that Mr. Weston would never marry again. Oh dear, no! Mr. Weston, who had been a widower so long, and who seemed so perfectly comfortable without a wife, so constantly occupied either in his business in town or among his friends here, always acceptable wherever he went, always cheerful—Mr. Weston need not spend a single evening in the year alone if he did not like it. Oh no! Mr. Weston certainly would never marry again. Some people even talked of a promise to his wife on her deathbed, and others of the son and the uncle not letting him. All manner of solemn nonsense was talked on the subject, but I believed none of it. Ever since the day (about four years ago) that Miss Taylor and I met with him in Broadway Lane, when, because it began to mizzle, he darted away with so much gallantry, and borrowed two umbrellas for us from Farmer Mitchell's, I made up my mind on the subject. I planned the match from that hour; and when such success has blessed me in this instance, dear papa, you cannot think that I shall leave off matchmaking."

Chapter 8

"I have reason to think," he replied, "that Harriet Smith will soon have an offer of marriage, and from a most unexceptionable quarter—Robert Martin is the man. Her visit to Abbey-Mill, this summer, seems to have done his business. He is desperately in love, and means to marry her."

"He is very obliging," said Emma; "but is he sure that Harriet means to marry him?" "Well, well, means to make her an offer, then. Will that do? He came to the Abbey two evenings ago, on purpose to consult me about it. He knows I have a thorough regard for him and all his family, and, I believe, considers me as one of his best friends. He came to ask me whether I thought it would be imprudent in him to settle so early; whether I thought her too young—in short, whether I approved his choice altogether; having some apprehension, perhaps, of her being considered (especially since your making so much of her) as in a line of society above him. I was very much pleased with all that he said. I never hear better sense from anyone than Robert Martin. He always speaks to the purpose; open, straightforward, and very well judging. He told me everything; his circumstances and plans, and what they all proposed doing in the event of his marriage. He is an excellent young man, both as son and brother. I had no hesitation in advising him to marry. He proved to me that he could afford it; and that being the case, I was convinced he could not do better. I praised the fair lady too, and altogether sent him away very happy. If he had never esteemed my opinion before, he would have thought highly of me then; and, I dare say, left the house thinking' me the best friend and counsellor man ever had. This happened the night before last. Now, as we may fairly suppose, he would not allow much time to pass before he spoke to the lady, and as he does not appear to have spoken yesterday, it is not unlikely that he should be at Mrs. Goddard's to-day; and she may be detained by a visitor, without thinking him at all a tiresome wretch." "Pray, Mr. Knightley," said Emma, who had been smiling to herself through a great part of this speech, "how do you know that Mr. Martin did not speak yesterday?" "Certainly," replied he, surprised, "I do not absolutely know it, but it may be inferred. Was not she the whole day with you?" "Come," said she, "I will tell you something in return for what you have told me. He did speak yesterday—that is, he wrote, and was refused." This was obliged to be repeated before it could be believed; and Mr. Knightley actually looked red with surprise and displeasure, as he stood up, in tall indignation, and said: "Then she is a greater simpleton than I ever believed her. What is the foolish girl about?" "Oh, to be sure," cried Emma, "it is always incomprehensible to a man, that a woman should ever refuse an offer of marriage. A man always imagines a woman to be ready for anybody who asks her." "Nonsense! A man does not imagine any such thing. But what is the meaning of this? Harriet Smith refuse Robert Martin! Madness, if it is so; but I hope you are mistaken." "I saw her answer! Nothing could be clearer." "You saw her answer! You wrote her answer too. Emma, this is your doing. You persuaded her to refuse him." "And if I did (which, however, I am far from allowing), I should not feel that I had done wrong. Mr. Martin is a very respectable young man, but I cannot admit him to be Harriet's equal; and am rather surprised, indeed, that he should have ventured to address her. By your account he does seem to have had some scruples. It is a pity that they were ever got over." "Not Harriet's equal!" exclaimed Mr. Knightley, loudly and warmly; and with calmer asperity added, a few moments afterwards, "No, he is not her equal, indeed, for he is as much her superior in sense as in situation. Emma, your infatuation about that girl blinds you. What are Harriet Smith's claims, either of birth, nature, or education, to any connection higher than Robert Martin? She is the natural daughter of nobody knows whom, with probably no settled provision at all, and certainly no respectable relations. She is known only as parlour boarder at a common school. She is not a sensible girl, nor a girl of any information. She has been taught nothing useful, and is too young and too simple to have acquired anything herself. At her age she can have no experience; and, with her little wit, is not very likely ever to have any that can avail her. She is pretty, and she is good-tempered, and that is all. My only scruple in advising the match was on his account, as being beneath his deserts, and a bad connection for him. I felt that, as to fortune, in all probability he might do much better, and that, as to a rational companion or useful helpmate, he could not do worse. But I could not reason so to a man in love, and was willing to trust to there being no harm in her; to her having that sort of disposition which, in good hands like his, might be easily led aright, and turn out very well. The advantage of the match I felt to be all on her side; and had not the smallest doubt (nor have I now) that there would be a general cry out upon her extreme good luck. Even your satisfaction I made sure of. It crossed my mind immediately that you would not regret your friend's leaving Highbury, for the sake of her being settled so well. I remember saying to myself, 'Even Emma, with all her partiality for Harriet, will think this a good match.'" "I cannot help wondering at your knowing so little of Emma as to say any such thing. What! Think a farmer (and with all his sense and all his merit Mr. Martin is nothing more) a good match for my intimate friend! Not regret her leaving Highbury, for the sake of marrying a man whom I could never admit as an acquaintance of my own! I wonder you should think it possible for me to have such feelings. I assure you mine are very different. I must think your statement by no means fair. You are not just to Harriet's Claims. They would be estimated very differently by others as well as myself; Mr. Martin may be the richest of the two, but he is undoubtedly her inferior as to rank in society. The sphere in which she moves is much above his. It would be a degradation." "A degradation to illegitimacy and ignorance to be married to a respectable, intelligent, gentleman-farmer!" "As to the circumstances of her birth, though in a legal sense she may be called Nobody, it will not hold in common sense. She is not to pay for the offence of others, by being held below the level of those with whom she is brought up. There can scarcely be a doubt that her father is a gentleman—and a gentleman of fortune. Her allowance is very liberal; nothing has ever been grudged for her improvement or comfort. That she is a gentleman's daughter is indubitable to me; that she associates with gentlemen's daughters, no one, I apprehend, will deny. She is superior to Mr. Robert Martin." "Whoever might be her parents," said Mr. Knightley, "whoever may have had the charge of her, it does not appear to have been any part of their plan to introduce her into what you would call good society. After receiving a very indifferent education, she is left in Mrs. Goddard's hands to shift as she can—to move, in short, in Mrs. Goddard's line, to have Mrs. Goddard's acquaintance. Her friends evidently thought this good enough for her; and it was good enough. She desired nothing better herself. Till you chose to turn her into a friend, her mind had no distaste for her own set, nor any ambition beyond it. She was as happy as possible with the Martins in the summer. She had no sense of superiority then. If she has it now, you have given it. You have been no friend to Harriet Smith, Emma. Robert Martin would never have proceeded so far, if he had not felt persuaded of her not being disinclined to him. I know him well. He has too much real feeling to address any woman on the haphazard of selfish passion. And as to conceit, he is the farthest from it of any man I know. Depend upon it, he had encouragement." It was most convenient to Emma not to make a direct reply to this assertion; she chose rather to take up her own line of the subject again.

Quoted from

http://vdisk.weibo.com/com/s/ta-Tsez8rIPE9.

Clip of the Movie

The part when Mr. Knightley and Emma talked about Harriet's feeling for Mr. Elton and Robert Martin, and whether they are suitable for Harriet or not.

Topics for Discussion

1. That Emma tries every means to make match for Harriet is the main clue of the novel. But in the movie, it seems that the producer focuses more on characters' emotional development simultaneously. Which way of narration is more appealing?

2. The Emma in the movie is less humble and embarrassed in the end than that in the novel due to the fame that the leading actress enjoys. Do you think this would put a damper on the understanding of the original novel?

Unit 2   Charles Dickens: *Great Expectations*

＼ Context

Despite any literary controversy over Dickens' style, most critics agree that *Great Expectations* is his best book. The story, while set in the early part of the 1800s, was written in 1860 during the Victorian era that began with the coronation of Queen Victoria in 1837 and lasted until her death in 1901. Virtues emphasized at that time included integrity, respectability, a sense of public duty, and maintaining a closeknit family. The period of the novel was a time of change. England was expanding worldwide and becoming a wealthy world power. The economy was changing from a mainly agricultural one to an industrial and trade–based one. While the world became more democratic, so, did literature. The people wanted characters, relationships, and social concerns that mattered to them, and they had the economic power to demand it. Dickens published *Great Expectations* in weekly installments that ran from December 1860 until August 1861. In keeping with the desire to please readers, Dickens, on the advice of a novelist friend, changed the ending of the story from a sad one to a happy one. The story has a three-part structure similar to that of a play, which is fitting, given that Dickens was involved in the theater for many years, writing, producing, and acting in plays. The plot is complicated and twisting, full of surprises and complexities.

＼ Plot

On Christmas Eve, around 1812, Pip, an orphan who is about seven years old, encounters an escaped convict in the village churchyard while visiting the graves of his mother, father and siblings. The convict scares Pip into stealing food and a file to grind away his shackles, from the home he shares with his abusive older sister and her kind husband Joe Gargery, a blacksmith. The next day, soldiers recapture the convict while he is engaged in a fight with another escaped convict; the two are returned to the prison ships.

Miss Havisham, a wealthy spinster who wears an old wedding dress and lives in the dilapidated Satis House, asks Pip's Uncle Pumblechook to find a boy to visit. Pip visits Miss Havisham and her adopted daughter Estella, falling in love with Estella on first sight, both quite young. Pip visits Miss Havisham regularly until it comes time for him to learn a trade; Joe accompanies Pip for the last visit when she gives the money for Pip to be bound as apprentice blacksmith. Pip settles into learning Joe's trade. When both are away from the house, Mrs. Joe is brutally attacked, leaving her unable to speak or do her work. Biddy arrives to help with her care and becomes "a blessing to the household".

Four years into Pip's apprenticeship, Mr. Jaggers, a lawyer, approaches him in the village with the news that he has expectations from an anonymous benefactor, with immediate funds to train him in the gentlemanly arts. He will not know the benefactor's name until that person speaks up. Pip is to leave for London in the proper clothes. He assumes that Miss Havisham is his benefactor. He visits her to say good-bye.

Pip sets up house with Herbert Pocket at Barnard's Inn. Herbert tells Pip the circumstances of Miss Havisham's romantic disappointment, her jilting by her fiancé. Pip goes to Hammersmith to be educated by Mr. Matthew Pocket, Herbert's father. Jaggers disburses the money Pip needs to set himself up in his new life. Joe visits Pip at Barnard's Inn, where Pip is a bit ashamed of Joe.

Joe relays the message from Miss Havisham that Estella will be at Satis House for a visit. Pip and Herbert exchange their romantic secrets—Pip adores Estella and Herbert is engaged to Clara.

Pip and Herbert build up debts. Mrs. Joe dies and Pip returns to his village for the funeral. Pip's income is fixed at £500 per annum when he comes of age at twenty-one. Pip takes Estella to Satis House. She and Miss Havisham quarrel. At the Assembly Ball in Richmond, Estella meets Bentley Drummle, a brute of a man. A week after he turns 23 years old, Pip learns that his benefactor is the convict from so long ago. Abel Magwitch, was transported to New South Wales after that escape. He became wealthy after gaining his freedom there. As long as he is out of England, Magwitch can live. But he returns to see Pip. Pip was his motivation for all his success in New South Wales. Pip is shocked, ceasing to take money from him. He and Herbert Pocket devise a plan to get Magwitch out of England, by boat. Magwitch shares his past history with Pip.

Pip tells Miss Havisham that he is as unhappy as she can ever have meant him to be. He asks her to finance Herbert Pocket. Estella tells Pip she will marry Bentley Drummle.

Miss Havisham tells Pip that Estella was brought to her by Jaggers aged two or three. Before Pip leaves the property, Miss Havisham accidentally sets her dress on fire. Pip saves her, injuring himself in the process. She eventually dies from her injuries, lamenting her manipulation of Estella and Pip. Jaggers tells Pip how he brought Estella to Miss Havisham from Molly. Pip figures out that Estella is the daughter of Molly and Magwitch.

A few days before the escape, Joe's former journeyman Orlick seizes Pip, confessing past crimes as he means to kill Pip. Herbert Pocket and Startop save Pip and prepare for the escape. On the river, they are met by a police boat carrying Compeyson for identification of Magwitch. Compeyson was the other convict years earlier, and as well, the con artist who wooed and deserted Miss Havisham. Magwitch seizes Compeyson, and they fight in the river. Magwitch survives to be taken by police, seriously injured. Compeyson's body is found later.

Pip visits Magwitch in jail and tells him that his daughter Estella is alive. Magwitch responds by squeezing Pip's palm and dies soon after sparing an execution. After Herbert goes to Cairo, Pip falls ill in his room. He is confronted with arrest for debt; he awakens to find Joe at his side. Joe nurses Pip back to health and pays off the debt. As Pip begins to walk about on his own, Joe slips away home. Pip returns to propose to Biddy, only to find that she and Joe have just married. Pip asks Joe for forgiveness, and Joe forgives him. As Magwitch's fortune in money and land was seized by the court, Pip no longer has income. Pip promises to repay Joe. Herbert asks him to join his firm in Cairo; he shares lodgings with Herbert and Clara and works as a clerk, advancing over time.

Eleven years later, Pip visits the ruins of Satis House and meets Estella, widow to the abusive Bentley Drummle. She asks Pip to forgive her, assuring him that misfortune has opened her heart and that she now empathizes with Pip. As Pip takes Estella's hand and leaves the ruins of Satis House, he sees "no shadow of another parting from her".

＼ Suggested Movie Version

The film is the seventh version of Charles Dickens's novel of the same name. David Nicholls was asked to develop the screenplay. Nicholls described in interviews that he saw Dickens's work as his childhood defining novel, having first read the book when he was fourteen and it having since remained his favorite. He also praised the 1946 version, directed by David Lean.

Mike Newell was looking to develop Dickens's *Dombey and Son* for the screen, but after it didn't go ahead, he was told about Nicholls's script. The two worked together on further developing the screenplay and finding the funding for the film. Nicholls thought there was a problem with choosing the ending for the film, as Dickens wrote both a downbeat ending and a more positive version. He described their solution as "What we've tried to do is to make it work as a love story without sentimentalizing the book", having criticized the ending of the David Lean version of the film.

＼ Important Quotations

Chapter 38

"I begin to think," said Estella, in a musing way, after another moment of calm wonder, "that I almost understand how this comes about. If you had brought up your adopted daughter wholly in the dark confinement of these rooms, and had never let her know that there was such a thing as the daylight by which she has never once seen your face—if you had done that, and then, for a purpose, had wanted her to understand the daylight and know all about it, you would have been disappointed and angry? ... "

"Or," said Estella, "—which is a nearer case—if you had taught her, from the dawn of her intelligence, with your utmost energy and might, that there was such a thing as daylight, but that it was made to be her enemy and destroyer, and she must always turn against it, for it had blighted you and would else blight her—if you had done this, and then, for a purpose, had wanted her to take naturally to the daylight and she could not do it, you would have been disappointed and angry? ... "

"So," said Estella, "I must be taken as I have been made. The success is not mine, the failure is not mine, but the two together make me."

Chapter 39

"Look'ee here, Pip. I'm your second father. You're my son—more to me nor any son. I've put away money, only for you to spend. When I was a hired-out shepherd in a solitary hut, not seeing no faces but faces of sheep till I half-forgot wot men's and women's faces wos like, I see yourn… I see you there a many times plain as ever I see you on them misty marshes. 'Lord strike me dead!' I says each time—and I goes out in the open air to say it under the open heavens—'but wot, if I gets liberty and money, I'll make that boy a gentleman!' And I done it. Why, look at you, dear boy! Look at these here lodgings of yourn, fit for a lord! A lord? Ah! You shall show money with lords for wagers, and beat' em!"

Chapter 56

"Dear Magwitch, I must tell you, now at last. You understand what I say?"

A gentle pressure on my hand.

"You had a child once, whom you loved and lost."

A stronger pressure on my hand.

"She lived and found powerful friends. She is living now. She is a lady and very beautiful. And I love her!"

Quoted from

http://novel.tingroom.com/html/book/show/78/.

Clip of The Movie

The part when Magwitch dramatically reveals himself as Pip's secret benefactor and the source of all his wealth.

Topics for Discussion

1. This movie, as the seventh version, puts more emphasis on a love story. Do you think it is compatible with the original novel?

2. If you were the playwright, would you choose the happy ending or the tragic ending? Why?

Chapter 5　The Brontë Sisters

Brontë, family of English novelists, including Charlotte Brontë (1816—1855), novelist, Emily Jane Brontë (1818—1848), novelist and poet, and Anne Brontë (1820—1849), novelist. The Brontë sisters were daughters of Patrick Brontë (1777—1861), an Anglican clergyman of Irish birth, educated at Cambridge. In 1820 Patrick Brontë became incumbent of Haworth, West Riding of Yorkshire. The next year his wife died, and her sister, Elizabeth Branwell, came to the parsonage to care for the six Brontë children, five girls and one boy, Branwell. Maria and Elizabeth, the two oldest girls, were sent to the Cowan Bridge school for the daughters of poor clergymen. In spite of the harsh conditions there, Charlotte and Emily were also sent in 1824, but were brought home after Maria and Elizabeth contracted tuberculosis and died. At home for the next five years, the children were left much to themselves, and they began to write about an imaginary world they had created. This escapist writing, transcribed in tiny script on small pieces of paper, continued into adulthood and is a remarkable key to the development of genius in Charlotte and Emily. In 1831, Charlotte was sent to Miss Wooler's school at Roe Head. She became a teacher there in 1835, but in 1838 she returned to Haworth. At home she found the family finances in wretched condition. Branwell—talented as a writer and painter, on whom his sisters' hopes for money and success rested—had lost three jobs and was declining into alcoholism and opium addiction. To increase their income Charlotte and her sisters laid ill-considered plans to establish a school. In order to study languages, Emily and Charlotte spent 1842 at the Pensionnat Héger in Brussels, but returned home at the death of their aunt, who had willed them her small fortune. Both girls were offered positions at the pensionnat, but only Charlotte returned in 1843. She went home the following year, because, it is thought, she was in love with Mr. Héger and had aroused the jealousy of Mme Héger. Mr. Brontë's failing eyesight and the rapid degeneration of Branwell made this an unhappy period at home. When Charlotte discovered Emily's poetry in 1845, Anne revealed hers, and the next year the collected poems of the three sisters, published at their own expense, appeared under the pseudonyms Currer, Ellis, and Acton Bell. In 1847 Emily's novel *Wuthering Heights* and Anne's *Agnes Grey* were published as a set. Although the novel *The Professor* by Charlotte was rejected, her *Jane Eyre* (1847) was accepted and published with great success. The identity of the sisters as authors was at first unknown even to their publishers. It was not until after the publication of Charlotte's *Shirley* in 1849 that the truth was made public. By the publication date tragedy had all but destroyed the Brontë family. In September 1848, Branwell died; Emily caught cold at his funeral and, refusing all medical aid, died of tuberculosis the following December. Anne, whose *Tenant of Wildfell Hall* appeared in 1848, also died of tuberculosis in May, 1849. Now that the people who had occupied most of her life were gone, Charlotte began to make trips to London where she was lionized. Her *Villette* appeared in 1853. In 1854 she married her father's curate, Arthur Bell Nichols, with whom she seems to have been happy. She died, however, of pregnancy toxemia complicated by the Brontë susceptibility to tuberculosis, after only a year of marriage. *The Professor* was published posthumously in 1857.

Context

Jane Eyre as an example:

When *Jane Eyre* was first published in 1847, it was an immediate popular and critical success. It also, however, met with criticism. In a famous attack in the *Quarterly Review* of December 1848, Elizabeth Rigby called Jane a "personification of an unregenerate and undisciplined spirit" and the novel as a whole, "anti-Christian." Rigby's critique perhaps accounts for some of the novel's continuing popularity: the rebelliousness of its tone. *Jane Eyre* calls into question most of society's major institutions, including education, family, social class, and Christianity. The novel asks the reader to consider a variety of contemporary social and political issues: What is women's position in society? What is the relation between Britain and its colonies? How important is artistic endeavor in human life? What is the relationship of dreams and fantasy to reality? And what is the basis of an effective marriage? Not just the story of the romance between Rochester and Jane, the novel also employs the conventions of the Bildungsroman, the gothic and the spiritual quest. For her, when one is closest to nature, one is also closest to God: "We read clearest His infinitude, His omnipotence, His omnipresence." God and nature are both sources of bounty, compassion and forgiveness.

Plot

Orphaned as an infant, Jane Eyre lives at Gateshead with her aunt, Sarah Reed, as the novel opens. Jane is sent to Lowood School, a charity institution for orphan girls, run by Mr. Brocklehurst. Despite the difficult conditions at Lowood, Jane prefers school to life with the Reeds. Here she makes two new friends: Miss Temple and Helen Burns. From Miss Temple, Jane learns proper ladylike behavior and compassion; from Helen she gains a more spiritual focus. The school's damp conditions, combined with the girls' near-starvation diet, produce a typhus epidemic, in which nearly half the students die, including Helen Burns, who dies in Jane's arms. Following this tragedy, Brocklehurst is deposed from his position as manager of Lowood, and conditions become more acceptable. Jane quickly becomes a star student, and after six years of hard work, an effective teacher. Following two years of teaching at Lowood, Jane is ready for new challenges. Miss Temple marries, and Lowood seems different without her. Jane places at advertisement for a governess position in the local newspaper. She receives only one reply, from a Mrs. Fairfax of Thornfield. Jane accepts the job. At Thornfield, a comfortable three-story country estate, Jane is warmly welcomed. Jane also discovers that Thornfield harbors a secret. From time to time, she hears strange, maniacal laughter coming from the third storey. One night, Jane smells smoke in the hallway, and realizes it is coming from

Rochester's room. Jane races down to his room, discovering his curtains and bed are on fire. Unable to wake Rochester, she douses both him and his bedding with cold water. He asks her not to tell anyone about this incident and blames the arson on Grace Poole. Why doesn't he press charges on Grace, or at least evict her from the house, Jane wonders. Following this incident, Rochester leaves suddenly for a house party at a local estate. Jane is miserable during his absence and realizes she is falling in love with him. After a weeklong absence, he returns with a party of guests, including the beautiful Blanche Ingram. Jane jealously believes Rochester is pursing this accomplished, majestic, dark-haired beauty. An old friend of Rochester's, Richard Mason, joins the party one day. From him, Jane learns that Rochester once lived in Spanish Town, Jamaica. One night, Mason is mysteriously attacked, supposedly by the crazy Grace Poole.

Later, Jane reveals her love for Rochester, and the two end up engaged. Jane is happy to be marrying the man she loves, but during the month before the wedding she is plagued by strange dreams of a destroyed Thornfield and a wailing infant. Two nights before the wedding, a frightening, dark-haired woman enters her room and rips her wedding veil in two. Although Jane is certain this woman didn't look like Grace Poole, Rochester assures her it must have been the bizarre servant. The morning of the wedding finally arrives. Jane and Rochester stand at the altar, taking their vows, when suddenly a strange man announces there's an impediment to the marriage: Rochester is already married to a woman named Bertha Antoinetta Mason. Rochester rushes the wedding party back to Thornfield, where they find his insane and repulsive wife locked in a room on the third storey. Grace Poole is the woman's keeper, but Bertha was responsible for the strange laughter and violence at Thornfield. Rochester tries to convince Jane to become his mistress and move with him to a pleasure villa in the south of France. Instead, herself sneaks away in the middle of the night, with little money and no extra clothing. With twenty shillings, the only money she has, she catches a coach that takes her to faraway Whitcross. On the third night, she follows a light that leads her across the moors to Marsh End, owned by the Rivers family. Hannah, the housekeeper, wants to send her away, but St. John Rivers, the clergyman who owns the house, offers her shelter. Jane soon becomes close friends with St. John's sisters, Diana and Mary. Furthermore, she discovers that St. John, his sisters, and herself are cousins. St. John plans to become a missionary in India. He tries to convince Jane to accompany him, as his wife. Jane leaves Moor House to search for her true love, Rochester. Arriving at Millcote, she discovers Thornfield a burned wreck, just as predicted in her dreams. From a local innkeeper, she learns that Bertha Mason burned the house down one night and that Rochester lost an eye and a hand while trying to save her and the servants. He now lives in seclusion at Ferndean. Jane immediately drives to Ferndean. There she discovers a powerless, unhappy Rochester. Jane carries a tray to him and reveals her identity. The two lovers are joyfully reunited and soon get married. Ten years later, Jane writes this narrative. Her married life is still blissful; Adele has grown to be a helpful companion for Jane; Diana and Mary Rivers are happily married; St. John still works as a missionary, but is nearing death; Rochester has regained partial vision, enough to see their first-born son.

Suggested Movie Version

Jane Eyre is a 2006 television adaptation of Charlotte Brontë's 1847 novel of the same name. The story, which has been the subject of numerous television and film adaptations, is based on the life of the orphaned titular character. This four-part BBC television drama serial adaptation was broadcast in the United Kingdom on BBC One.

The mini-series is generally considered a successful adaptation, garnering critical acclaim and a number of prestigious nominations from various award bodies.

Important Quotations

Chapter 4

I am glad you are no relation of mine. I will never call you aunt again as long as I live. I will never come to visit you when I am grown up; and if anyone asks me how I liked you, and how you treated me, I will say the very thought of you makes me sick, and that you treated me with miserable cruelty... You think I have no feelings, and that I can do without one bit of love or kindness; but I cannot live so: and you have no pity. I shall remember how you thrust me back...into the red-room... And that punishment you made me suffer because your wicked boy struck me—knocked me down for nothing. I will tell anybody who asks me questions this exact tale. 'Ere I had finished this reply, my soul began to expand, to exult, with the strangest sense of freedom, of triumph, I ever felt. It seemed as if an invisible bond had burst, and that I had struggled out into unhoped-for liberty...

Chapter 34

"Shall I?" I said briefly; and I looked at his features, beautiful in their harmony, but strangely formidable in their still severity; at his brow, commanding, but not open; at his eyes, bright and deep and searching, but never soft; at his tall imposing figure; and fancied myself in idea his wife. Oh! it would never do! As his curate, his comrade, all would be right: I would cross oceans with him in that capacity; toil under Eastern suns, in Asian deserts with him in that office; admire and emulate his courage and devotion and vigour: accommodate quietly to his masterhood; smile undisturbed at his ineradicable ambition... I should suffer often, no doubt, attached to him only in this capacity: my body would be under a rather stringent yoke, but my heart and mind would be free. I should still have my unblighted self to turn to: my natural unenslaved feelings with which to communicate in moments of loneliness. There would be recesses in my mind which would be only mine, to which he never came; and sentiments growing there, fresh and sheltered, which his austerity could never blight, nor his measured warrior-march trample down: but as his wife—at his side always, and always restrained, and always checked—forced to keep the fire of my nature continually low, to compel it to burn inwardly and never utter a cry, though the imprisoned flame consumed vital after vital—this would be unendurable.

Final Passage

I have now been married ten years. I know what it is to live entirely for and with what I love best on earth. I hold myself supremely blest—blest beyond what language can express; because I am my husband's life as fully as he is mine. No woman was ever nearer to her mate than I am: ever more absolutely bone of his bone, and flesh of his flesh. I know no weariness of my Edward's society: he knows none of mine, any more than we each do of the pulsation of the heart that beats in our separate bosoms; consequently, we are ever together. To be together is for us to be at once as free as in solitude, as gay as in company. We talk, I believe, all day long: to talk to each other is but a more animated and an audible thinking. All my confidence is bestowed on him, all his confidence is devoted to me; we are precisely suited in character—perfect concord is the result.

Quoted from

http://vdisk.weibo.com/s/dzgkuq3_Glq4H.

Clip of the Movie

The part when Jane Eyre returns to Thornfield, and finds a weakened and blind Rochester and a burnt down Thornfield. The two are married and the entire family "—" Rochester, Jane, Adele, St. John Rivers' sisters, two children, and the dog Pilot "—" gather in the garden to have their portrait painted.

Topics for Discussion

1. While for the most part a faithful retelling of the novel, the screenplay does contain minor deviations. The middle of the novel is instead developed and a few scenes from the novel are compressed or moved to different times and places in the narrative. Additional scenes were created for the screenplay which underscore the passionate natures of Jane and Rochester. So, would the deviations have a negative impact on the characterization and the expression of the themes?

2. Should film playwright deliberately cater to the audience's taste in order to increase the box-office revenues?

Chapter 6　Henry James: *Daisy Miller*

﹨ Context

Henry James (1843—1916) grew up mostly in the US but spent most of his life in England. In 1855, the James started a three-year trip to European countries, which impressed Henry so much that in 1915 he became a British citizen. During his youth, James came to know many of literary greats of the time because of his family's prominence. As one of the most important literary writers in the late 19th century, James produced lots of novels, articles, and literary criticism. He insisted that a text should be realistic. Among his novels, *Daisy Miller* (1879), *The Portrait of a Lady* (1881), *The Bostonians* (1886), and *The Ambassadors* (1903) are good examples of his major theme showing the clash between the corruption of the old and the innocent of the New World.

Daisy Miller was based on a gossip that Henry James got from his female friend, Alice Bartlett. She told him about a young American girl who visited Rome in a winter day and met a good-looking Roman. Based on this gossip, James dramatized it and sent it to an English editor and made it published first in London and later in the US. The novella was very successful and aroused great attention from the public. *Daisy Miller* has been praised as the first "international novel".

﹨ Plot

Mr. Winterbourne, a young American, meets a rich, pretty American girl Daisy Miller at a hotel in Vevey, Switzerland. In Winterbourne's eyes, Daisy is quite different from other European girls for her being "uncultivated". Mr. Winterbourne spends some time with Daisy going to local tourist attractions. Next winter, Mr. Winterbourne goes to Rome and knows that Daisy has become the talk of the town, especially her relationship with a handsome Italian, Mr. Giovanelli, which scandalizes the American community in Rome. Later, Daisy becomes seriously ill because of her exposure to "Roman fever" and dies soon. Before she dies, she gives the message to Mr. Winterbourne that she cares much what he thinks about her. At that time, Mr. Winterbourne realizes that he should go back to the natural life instead of the old style of life in Europe.

﹨ Suggested Movie Version

The 1974 film version of *Daisy Miller* was produced and directed by American director Peter Bogdanovich. It spelled the beginning of the end of Bogdanovich's career as a popular, critically acclaimed director. His girlfriend Cybill Shepherd at that time starred as Daisy Miller but was criticized harshly. Barry Brown, a young actor who later shot himself to death at the age of 27, starred Winterbourne in the film.

✎ Important Quotations

Part II

When, on his return from the villa (it was eleven o'clock), Winterbourne approached the dusky circle of the Colosseum, it recurred to him, as a lover of the picturesque, that the interior, in the pale moonshine, would be well worth a glance. He turned aside and walked to one of the empty arches, near which, as he observed, an open carriage—one of the little Roman streetcabs—was stationed. Then he passed in, among the cavernous shadows of the great structure, and emerged upon the clear and silent arena. The place had never seemed to him more impressive. One-half of the gigantic circus was in deep shade; the other was sleeping in the luminous dusk. As he stood there he began to murmur Byron's famous lines, out of "Manfred," but before he had finished his quotation he remembered that if nocturnal meditations in the Colosseum are recommended by the poets, they are deprecated by the doctors. The historic atmosphere was there, certainly; but the historic atmosphere, scientifically considered, was no better than a villainous miasma. Winterbourne walked to the middle of the arena, to take a more general glance, intending thereafter to make a hasty retreat. The great cross in the center was covered with shadow; it was only as he drew near it that he made it out distinctly. Then he saw that two persons were stationed upon the low steps which formed its base. One of these was a woman, seated; her companion was standing in front of her.

Presently the sound of the woman's voice came to him distinctly in the warm night air. "Well, he looks at us as one of the old lions or tigers may have looked at the Christian martyrs!" These were the words he heard, in the familiar accent of Miss Daisy Miller.

"Let us hope he is not very hungry," responded the ingenious Giovanelli. "He will have to take me first; you will serve for dessert!"

Winterbourne stopped, with a sort of horror, and, it must be added, with a sort of relief. It was as if a sudden illumination had been flashed upon the ambiguity of Daisy's behavior, and the riddle had become easy to read. She was a young lady whom a gentleman need no longer be at pains to respect. He stood there, looking at her—looking at her companion and not reflecting that though he saw them vaguely, he himself must have been more brightly visible. He felt angry with himself that he had bothered so much about the right way of regarding Miss Daisy Miller. Then, as he was going to advance again, he checked himself, not from the fear that he was doing her injustice, but from a sense of the danger of appearing unbecomingly exhilarated by this sudden revulsion from cautious criticism. He turned away toward the entrance of the place, but, as he did so, he heard Daisy speak again.

"Why, it was Mr. Winterbourne! He saw me, and he cuts me!"

What a clever little reprobate she was, and how smartly she played at injured innocence! But he wouldn't cut her. Winterbourne came forward again and went toward the great cross. Daisy had got up; Giovanelli lifted his hat. Winterbourne had now begun to think simply of the craziness, from a sanitary point of view, of a delicate young girl lounging away the evening in this nest of malaria. What if she WERE a clever little reprobate? That was no reason for her dying of the perniciosa.

Quoted from

http://www.pagebypagebooks.com/Henry_James/Daisy_Miller/Part_II_p17.html.

Clip of the Movie

The part of the night when Winterbourne met Daisy and Giovanelli nearby the Colosseum.

Topics for Discussion

1. Imagine what the psychological state of Daisy Miller was in when she saw Winterbourne at the night nearby the Colosseum.

2. In what way does Daisy's relationship with Mr. Giovanelli differ from that with Winterbourne?

3. What's Henry James's portrait of Daisy Miller? Some critics think it's Henry James's insult to Americans. Do you agree? Why or why not?

Chapter 7　E. M. Forster: *A Room with a View*

❚ Context

Edward Morgan Forster was a graduate from Cambridge University in 1901. Raised by his mother and aunt, he prefers to show strong female characters in his novels. He traveled in Italy, Greece, Germany and other countries while writing novels. *A Room with a View* (1908) was produced while he stayed in Italy. *Howard's End* (1910) was published and greatly acclaimed by the public. And *A Passage to India* (1924) was also a great success though considered as his "most complex and mature work". Forster, almost in his writings, shows his favor for new, liberal social behaviors of the Edwardian age, much more than the sober ideals during Queen Victoria's reign. As an active member of the Bloomsbury Group, Forster shared radical opposition to Victorian traditions and manners with other members of the Group such as Virginia Woolf and John Maynard Keynes.

A Room with a View tells a story about a young English woman, Lucy, in an Edwardian era of England. With the trip of Lucy to Italy, the story is set both in Italy and England, with love story and critique of the English society and presentation of the Italian view.

❚ Plot

Lucy Honeychurch, a young English woman, is touring Florence, Italy with her older cousin Charlotte Bartlett. While complaining that they are given rooms that look into the courtyard instead of the river Arno, Charlotte and Lucy are offered generously by Mr. Emerson and his son George rooms with view of the river. The following days in Florence is marked by Lucy's several encounters with the Emersons, especially George's kisses for Lucy. When Lucy comes back home in Surrey, England, she accepts Cecil Vyse's third-time proposal. Cecil has a small ugly villa for rent in the town. By chance, Cecil meets the Emersons in a museum and rents the villa to the father and the son. George again kisses Lucy in a moment alone and tells her that Cecil is not the right man for her. Lucy decides to break off her engagement with Cecil. However, puzzled with her own feeling, Lucy decides to travel to Greece with two elderly women. By chance again, she meets old Mr. Emerson and realizes her love towards George. The couple get married and stay happily at the end in Florence again in a room with a view.

❚ Suggested Movie Version

A Room with a View (1985) was directed by James Ivory and produced by Ismail Merchant based on E. M. Forster's novel. Ruth Prawer Jhabvala wrote the screenplay (the three are always regarded as Merchant-Ivory banner). In 1987, this film won 3 Oscar awards for Best Writing, Best

A Room with a View

Art Direction and Best Costume Design, and also another 23 wins and 21 nominations.

Maggie Smith played the role of Charlotte Bartlett. As one of the world's most famous and distinguished actresses, she has performed in over 60 films and television series. She is the formidable Professor McGonagall in films of *Harry Potter* and also Dowager Countess of Grantham in *Downton Abbey*. Helena Bonham Carter who played the role of Lucy Honeychurch, is also an actress of great versatility and is regarded as one of the UK's finest and most successful actresses. She had roles in three other productions under the Merchant-Ivory banner, such as *Maurice* (1987), *Where the Angels Fear to Tread* (1991) and *Howard's End* (1992).

＼ Important Quotations

Chapter 15

Ah, how beautiful the Weald looked! The hills stood out above its radiance, as Fiesole stands above the Tuscan Plain, and the South Downs, if one chose, were the mountains of Carrara. She might be forgetting her Italy, but she was noticing more things in her England. One could play a new game with the view, and try to find in its innumerable folds some town or village that would do for Florence. Ah, how beautiful the Weald looked!

But now Cecil claimed her. He chanced to be in a lucid critical mood, and would not sympathize with exaltation. He had been rather a nuisance all through the tennis, for the novel that he was reading was so bad that he was obliged to read it aloud to others. He would stroll round the precincts of the court and call out: "I say, listen to this, Lucy. Three split infinitives."

"Dreadful!" said Lucy, and missed her stroke. When they had finished their set, he still went on reading; there was some murder scene, and really every one must listen to it. Freddy and Mr. Floyd were obliged to hunt for a lost ball in the laurels, but the other two acquiesced.

"The scene is laid in Florence."

"What fun, Cecil! Read away. Come, Mr. Emerson, sit down after all your energy." She had "forgiven" George, as she put it, and she made a point of being pleasant to him.

He jumped over the net and sat down at her feet asking: "You—and are you tired?"

"Of course I'm not!"

"Do you mind being beaten?"

She was going to answer, "No," when it struck her that she did mind, so she answered, "Yes." She added merrily, "I don't see you're such a splendid player, though. The light was behind you, and it was in my eyes."

"I never said I was."

"Why, you did!"

"You didn't attend."

"You said—oh, don't go in for accuracy at this house. We all exaggerate, and we get very angry with people who don't."

"'The scene is laid in Florence,'" repeated Cecil, with an upward note.

Lucy recollected herself.

"'Sunset. Leonora was speeding—'"

Lucy interrupted. "Leonora? Is Leonora the heroine? Who's the book by?"

"Joseph Emery Prank. 'Sunset. Leonora speeding across the square. Pray the saints she might not arrive too late. Sunset—the sunset of Italy. Under Orcagna's Loggia—the Loggia de' Lanzi, as we sometimes call it now—'"

Lucy burst into laughter. "'Joseph Emery Prank' indeed! Why it's Miss Lavish! It's Miss Lavish's novel, and she's publishing it under somebody else's name."

"Who may Miss Lavish be?"

"Oh, a dreadful person—Mr. Emerson, you remember Miss Lavish?"

Excited by her pleasant afternoon, she clapped her hands.

George looked up. "Of course I do. I saw her the day I arrived at Summer Street. It was she who told me that you lived here."

"Weren't you pleased?" She meant "to see Miss Lavish," but when he bent down to the grass without replying, it struck her that she could mean something else. She watched his head, which was almost resting against her knee, and she thought that the ears were reddening. "No wonder the novel's bad," she added. "I never liked Miss Lavish. But I suppose one ought to read it as one's met her."

"All modern books are bad," said Cecil, who was annoyed at her inattention, and vented his annoyance on literature. "Everyone writes for money in these days."

"Oh, Cecil—!"

"It is so. I will inflict Joseph Emery Prank on you no longer."

Cecil, this afternoon seemed such a twittering sparrow. The ups and downs in his voice were noticeable, but they did not affect her. She had dwelt amongst melody and movement, and her nerves refused to answer to the clang of his. Leaving him to be annoyed, she gazed at the black head again. She did not want to stroke it, but she saw herself wanting to stroke it; the sensation was curious.

"How do you like this view of ours, Mr. Emerson?"

"I never notice much difference in views."

"What do you mean?"

"Because they're all alike. Because all that matters in them is distance and air."

"H'm!" said Cecil, uncertain whether the remark was striking or not.

"My father"—he looked up at her (and he was a little flushed)—"says that there is only one perfect view—the view of the sky straight over our heads, and that all these views on earth are but bungled copies of it."

"I expect your father has been reading Dante," said Cecil, fingering the novel, which alone permitted him to lead the conversation.

"He told us another day that views are really crowds—crowds of trees and houses and hills—and are bound to resemble each other, like human crowds—and that the power they have over us is sometimes supernatural, for the same reason."

Lucy's lips parted.

"For a crowd is more than the people who make it up. Something gets added to it—no one knows how—just as something has got added to those hills."

He pointed with his racquet to the South Downs.

"What a splendid idea!" she murmured. "I shall enjoy hearing your father talk again. I'm so sorry he's not so well."

"No, he isn't well."

"There's an absurd account of a view in this book," said Cecil. "Also that men fall into two classes—those who forget views and those who remember them, even in small rooms."

"Mr. Emerson, have you any brothers or sisters?"

"None. Why?"

"You spoke of 'us.' "

"My mother, I was meaning."

Cecil closed the novel with a bang.

"Oh, Cecil—how you made me jump!"

"I will inflict Joseph Emery Prank on you no longer."

"I can just remember us all three going into the country for the day and seeing as far as Hindhead. It is the first thing that I remember."

Cecil got up; the man was ill-bred—he hadn't put on his coat after tennis—he didn't do. He would have strolled away if Lucy had not stopped him.

"Cecil, do read the thing about the view."

"Not while Mr. Emerson is here to entertain us."

"No—read away. I think nothing's funnier than to hear silly things read out loud. If Mr. Emerson thinks us frivolous, he can go."

This struck Cecil as subtle, and pleased him. It put their visitor in the position of a prig. Somewhat mollified, he sat down again.

"Mr. Emerson, go and find tennis balls." She opened the book. Cecil must have his reading and anything else that he liked. But her attention wandered to George's mother, who—according to Mr. Eager—had been murdered in the sight of God according to her son—had seen as far as Hindhead.

"Am I really to go?" asked George.

"No, of course not really," she answered.

"Chapter two," said Cecil, yawning. "Find me chapter two, if it isn't bothering you."

Chapter two was found, and she glanced at its opening sentences.

She thought she had gone mad.

"Here—hand me the book."

She heard her voice saying: "It isn't worth reading—it's too silly to read—I never saw such rubbish—it oughtn't to be allowed to be printed."

He took the book from her.

"'Leonora,'" he read, "'sat pensive and alone. Before her lay the rich champaign of Tuscany, dotted over with many a smiling village. The season was spring.'"

Miss Lavish knew, somehow, and had printed the past in draggled prose, for Cecil to read and for George to hear.

"'A golden haze,'" he read. He read, "'Afar off the towers of Florence, while the bank on which she sat was carpeted with violets. All unobserved Antonio stole up behind her—'"

Lest Cecil should see her face she turned to George and saw his face.

He read: "'There came from his lips no wordy protestation such as formal lovers use. No eloquence was his, nor did he suffer from the lack of it. He simply enfolded her in his manly arms.'"

"This isn't the passage I wanted," he informed them. "there is another much funnier, further on." He turned over the leaves.

"Should we go in to tea?" said Lucy, whose voice remained steady.

She led the way up the garden, Cecil following her, George last. She thought a disaster was averted. But when they entered the shrubbery it came. The book, as if it had not worked mischief enough, had been forgotten, and Cecil must go back for it; and George, who loved passionately, must blunder against her in the narrow path.

"No—" she gasped, and, for the second time, was kissed by him.

As if no more was possible, he slipped back; Cecil rejoined her; they reached the upper lawn alone.

Quoted from

http://pd.sparknotes.com/lit/room/section15.html.

Clip of the Movie

The part when George was invited to play tennis with the Honeychurches. Less interested in Cecil's book, George and Lucy enjoyed more about the beautiful view from Windy Corner. On the way to the teahouse, George kissed Lucy.

Topics for Discussion

1. The film version of 1985 is always regarded as a well-adapted one. How do you like it? Are Lucy and George up to your imagination? Why or why not?

2. There are a lot of depictions both in the novel and in the film about the nature. What do you think of the role of nature?

3. Compare Italy and England in this novel. How does the life in England compared with that in Italy?

Chapter 8　Orwell: *Animal Farm*

Context

As Orwell spent more and more time with the down-and-outs of England, he became convinced that the only remedy for the invidious problem of poverty lay in socialism, a political and economic philosophy arguing that only when the state controls the means of production and distribution will all members of a nation share its profits and rewards. As he explained in his Preface to the Ukrainian edition of *Animal Farm*, "I became pro-Socialist more out of disgust with the way the poorer section of the industrial workers were oppressed and neglected than out of any theoretical admiration for a planned society." His detestation and fear of totalitarianism thus informed much of his literary output. Orwell examined socialism in a number of his nonfiction works but was prompted to write *Animal Farm* by what he saw as a prevalent belief that the Russian Revolution of 1917 was a step toward socialism for millions of poor and oppressed Russians. Orwell felt that Stalin's brutal rise to power was not only barbaric, but a betrayal of the socialist principles for which Lenin, Trotsky, and he had presumably revolted. Orwell began thinking about how he could best communicate his opinions on socialism and Stalin. His thoughts were ignited when he happened to see a village boy whipping a cart-horse. At that moment, Orwell received the inspiration he needed to formulate his ideas into *Animal Farm*, as the government in a totalitarian state exploits the common people. "It struck me that if only such animals became aware of their strength, we would have no power over them, and that men exploit animals." Now Orwell had a plan for his novel which would both argue the need for a true socialist government and warn the world of the ways in which socialist ideas threatened the will of these in power who wish to control other people. After a number of rejections from publishers, the novel was finally accepted by the small publishing firm of Secker and Warburg and proved to be a tremendous success, both in England and the United States. After *Nineteen Eighty-Four*, another novel that portrays life under an oppressive government, *Animal Farm* is Orwell's most renowned work. The novel asks its readers to examine the ways in which political leaders with seemingly noble and altruistic motives can betray the very ideals in which they ostensibly believe, as well as the ways in which certain members of a nation can elect themselves to positions of great power and abuse their fellow citizens, all under the guise of assisting them. Orwell describes *Animal Farm* as "the first book in which I tried, with full consciousness of what I was doing, to fuse political purpose and artistic purpose into one whole". Orwell felt that a farm where "All Animals Are Equal" would solve many social and economic problems—but he also knew that such a system would be difficult to maintain.

Plot

One night, all the animals at Mr. Jones' Manor Farm assemble in a barn to hear old Major, a pig, describe a dream he had about a world where all animals live free from the tyranny of their human masters. Old Major dies soon after the meeting, but the animals—inspired by his philosophy of Animalism—plot a rebellion against Jones. Two pigs, Snowball and Napoleon, prove themselves important figures and planners of this dangerous enterprise. When Jones forgets to feed the animals, the revolution occurs, and Jones and his men are chased off the farm. Manor Farm is renamed Animal Farm, and the Seven Commandments of Animalism are painted on the barn wall. Initially, the rebellion is a success. Napoleon, however, proves to be a power-hungry leader. Later that fall, Jones and his men return to Animal Farm and attempt to retake it. Snowball begins drawing plans for a windmill, which will provide electricity and thereby give the animals more leisure time, but Napoleon vehemently opposes such a plan on the grounds that building the windmill will allow them less time for producing food. On the Sunday that the pigs offer the windmill to the animals for a vote, Napoleon summons a pack of ferocious dogs, who chase Snowball off the farm forever. Napoleon announces that there will be no further debates; he also tells them that the windmill will be built after all and lies that it was his own idea, stolen by Snowball. For the rest of the novel, Napoleon uses Snowball as a scapegoat on whom he blames all of the animals' hardships. Contrary to the principles of Animalism, Napoleon hires a solicitor and begins trading with neighboring farms. Napoleon's lust for power increases to the point where he becomes a totalitarian dictator. Frederick and his men attack the farm and explode the windmill but are eventually defeated. As more of the Seven Commandments of Animalism are broken by the pigs, the language of the Commandments is revised. Years pass and Animal Farm expands its boundaries after Napoleon purchases two fields from another neighboring farmer, Pilkington. The novel ends with Pilkington sharing drinks with the pigs in Jones' house. Napoleon changes the name of the farm back to Manor Farm and quarrels with Pilkington during a card game in which both of them try to play the ace of spades. As other animals watch the scene from outside the window, they cannot tell the pigs from the humans.

Suggested Movie Version

Animal Farm is a 1954 British animated drama film by Halas and Batchelor, based on the book *Animal Farm* by George Orwell. It was the first British animated feature to be released. The C.I.A. paid for the filming, part of the U.S. cultural offensive during the Cold War, and influenced how Orwell's ideas were to be presented.

The "financial backers" influenced the development of the film—the altered ending, and that the message should be that, "Stalin's regime is not only as bad as Jones's, but worse and more cynical", and Napoleon "not only as bad as JONES but vastly worse". And the "investors" were greatly concerned that Snowball was presented too sympathetically in early script treatments and that Batchelor's script implied Snowball was "intelligent, dynamic, courageous". This implication could not be permitted. A memo declared that Snowball must be presented as a "fanatic intellectual whose plans if carried through would have led to disaster no less complete than under Napoleon".

❧ Important Quotations

Chapter I

Beasts of England, beasts of Ireland,

Beasts of every land and clime,

Hearken to my joyful tiding

Of the golden future time.

The Seven Commandments of Animalism in Chapter III

Whatever goes upon two legs is an enemy.

Whatever goes upon four legs, or has wings, is a friend.

No animal shall wear clothes.

No animal shall sleep in a bed.

No animal shall drink alcohol.

No animal shall kill any other animal.

All animals are equal.

Chapter X

All animals are equal, but some animals are more equal than others.

Quoted from

http://www.en8848.com.cn/fiction/fiction/classic/765.html.

Clip of the Movie

The part when the animals looked at the Seven Commandments of Animalism.

Topics for Discussion

1. The movie and the novel's endings are different. What do you think of this? Would this reduce the ironical tone in the original novel?

2. Are there any differences between the representative animal characters in the movie and the novel? In the movie, Snowball is not highlighted. Why?

Chapter 9　Fowles: *The French Lieutenant's Woman*

＼Context

This novel is based on the nineteenth-century romantic or gothic novel, a literary genre which can trace its origins back to the eighteenth century. Although Fowles perfectly reproduces typical characters, situations, and even dialogue, the reader should always be aware of the irony inherent in Fowles' perception; for his perspective, however cleverly disguised, is that of the twentieth century. We see this both in the authorial intrusions, which comment on the mores of people in Victorian England, and in his choice of opening quotations, which are drawn from the writings of people whose observations belie the assumptions that most Victorians held about their world. Fowles is concerned in this novel with the effects of society on the individual's awareness of himself or herself and how that awareness dominates and distorts his or her entire life, including relationships with other people. All the main characters in this novel are molded by what they believe to be true about themselves and others. In this case, their lives are governed by what the Victorian Age thought was true about the nature of men and women and their relationships to each other. *The French Lieutenant's Woman* of the title, for example, is the dark, mysterious woman of the typical Victorian romantic novel. Sometimes the villainess, sometimes the heroine, such a woman was a symbol of what was forbidden. It is this aura of strangeness about Sarah Woodruff that first attracts Charles Smithson's attention. The story that develops around this pair echoes other romantic novels of a similar type, wherein a man falls in love with a strange and sometimes evil woman. Charles's relationship with Ernestina Freeman creates another sort of romantic story, one that formed the basis of many Victorian novels. In the present story, the romantic situation which develops around the pair of aristocratic young people is not allowed to prevail over the forces, including the dark lady, that would normally keep Charles and Ernestina apart. Thus Fowles uses the popularity of the comedy of manners and combines it with the drama and sensationalism of the gothic novel and, using several stylistic conventions, creates a masterful, many-layered mystery that is one of the finest pieces of modern literature.

＼Plot

Set in the mid-nineteenth century, the narrator identifies the novel's protagonist as Sarah Woodruff, the "Woman" of the title, also known as "Tragedy" or "The French Lieutenant's Whore". She lives in the coastal town of Lyme Regis as a disgraced woman, supposedly abandoned by a French ship's officer named Varguennes who had returned to France and married. She spends some of her limited free time on the Cobb, a stone jetty where she stares out the sea.

One day, Charles Smithson, an orphaned gentleman, and Ernestina Freeman, his fiancée and a daughter of a wealthy tradesman, see Sarah walking along the cliffside. Ernestina tells Charles something of Sarah's story, and he becomes curious about her. Though continuing to court Ernestina, Charles has several more encounters with Sarah, meeting her clandestinely three times. During these meetings, Sarah tells Charles of her history, and asks for his emotional and social support. During the same period, he learns of the possible loss of place as heir to his elderly uncle, who has become engaged to a woman young enough to bear a child. Meanwhile, Charles' servant Sam falls in love with Mary, the maid of Ernestina's aunt.

In fact, Charles has fallen in love with Sarah and advises her to leave Lyme for Exeter. Returning from a journey to warn Ernestina's father about his uncertain inheritance, Charles stops in Exeter as if to visit Sarah. From there, the narrator, who intervenes throughout the novel and later becomes a character in it, offers three different ways in which the novel could end:

First ending: Charles does not visit Sarah, but immediately returns to Lyme to reaffirm his love for Ernestina. They marry, though the marriage never becomes particularly happy, and Charles enters trade under Ernestina's father, Mr. Freeman. The narrator pointedly notes the lack of knowledge about Sarah's fate. Charles tells Ernestina about an encounter which he implies is with the "French Lieutenant's Whore", but elides the sordid details, and the matter is ended. The narrator dismisses this ending as a daydream by Charles, before the alternative events of the subsequent meeting with Ernestina are described. Critic Michelle Phillips Buchberger describes this first ending as "a semblance of verisimilitude in the traditional 'happy ending'" found in actual Victorian novels.

Before the second and third endings, the narrator appears as a character sharing a railway compartment with Charles. He tosses a coin to determine the order in which he will portray the other two possible endings, emphasizing their equal plausibility. They are as follows.

Second ending: Charles and Sarah have a rash sexual encounter in which Charles realizes that Sarah was a virgin. Reflecting on his emotions during this, Charles ends his engagement to Ernestina, and proposes to Sarah through a letter. Charles's servant Sam fails to deliver the letter and, after Charles breaks his engagement, Ernestina's father disgraces him. His uncle marries and his wife bears an heir, ensuring the loss of the expected inheritance. To escape the social suicide and depression caused by his broken engagement, Charles goes abroad to Europe and America. Ignorant of Charles' proposal, Sarah flees to London without telling her lover. During Charles's trips abroad, his lawyer searches for Sarah, finding her two years later living in the Chelsea house of the painter and poet Dante Gabriel Rossetti, where she enjoys an artistic, creative life. Sarah shows Charles the child of their affair, leaving him in hope that the three may be reunited.

Third ending: The narrator re-appears outside the house at 16 Cheyne Walk and turns back his pocket watch by fifteen minutes. Events are the same as in the second-ending version until Charles meets Sarah, when their reunion is sour. The new ending does not make clear the parentage of the child and Sarah expresses no interest in reviving the relationship. Charles leaves the house, intending to return to the United States, wondering whether Sarah is a manipulative, lying woman who exploited him.

Suggested Movie Version

 The film intercuts the stories of two affairs: one is a Victorian period drama involving the gentleman palaeontologist Charles Smithson and the complex and troubled Sarah Woodruff, "The French Lieutenant's Woman"; the other is between the actors "Mike" and "Anna", playing the lead roles in a modern filming of the story. In both segments, Jeremy Irons and Meryl Streep play the lead roles, but in line with John Fowles' source novel having multiple endings, the two otherwise parallel stories have different outcomes.

Important Quotations

Chapter 2

She turned to look at him—or as it seemed to Charles, through him. It was not so much what was positively in that face which remained with him after that first meeting, but all that was not as he had expected; for theirs was an age when the favored feminine look was the demure, the obedient, the shy. Charles felt immediately as if he had trespassed; as if the Cobb belonged to that face, and not to the Ancient Borough of Lyme. It was not a pretty face, like Ernestina's. It was certainly not a beautiful face, by any period's standard or taste. But it was an unforgettable face, and a tragic face. Its sorrow welled out of it as purely, naturally and unstoppably as water out of a woodland spring. There was no artifice there, no hypocrisy, no hysteria, no mask; and above all, no sign of madness. The madness was in the empty sea, the empty horizon, the lack of reason for such sorrow; as if the spring was natural in itself, but unnatural in welling from a desert.

Again and again, afterwards, Charles thought of that look as a lance; and to think so is of course not merely to describe an object but the effect it has. He felt himself in that brief instant an unjust enemy; both pierced and deservedly diminished. The woman said nothing. Her look back lasted two or three seconds at most; then she resumed her stare to the south. Ernestina plucked Charles, sleeve, and he turned away, with a shrug and a smile at her. When they were nearer land he said, "I wish you hadn't told me the sordid facts. That's the trouble with provincial life. Everyone knows everyone and there is no mystery. No romance."

She teased him then: the scientist, the despiser of novels.

Chapter 13

I do not know. This story I am telling is all imagination. These characters I create never existed outside my own mind. If I have pretended until now to know my characters' minds and innermost thoughts, it is because I am writing in a convention universally accepted at the time of my story: that the novelist stands next to God.

Quoted from

http://novel.tingroom.com/jingdian/384/9817.html. (Chapter 2)

http://nonel.tingroom.con/jingdian/384/9828.html. (Chapter 13)

Clip of the Movie

The part when Charles met Sarah for the first time on the Cobb.

Topics for Discussion

1. Why does Fowles give the novel two conclusions? Do you consider them to be equally viable options, or is one more of a conclusion than the other?

2. Do you agree with the statement that the novelist stands next to God? Why or why not?

Chapter 10   McEwan: *Atonement*

﹨ Context

As one of the most famous English novelists in UK now, Ian R. McEwan (1948—) has been on the list of "The 50 greatest British writers since 1945" in 2008 by *The Times*. Ian started his writing career with Gothic short stories which earned him a nickname "Ian Macabre". Later he produced several novels which are all successful. *Enduring Love* (1997) was adapted into film and *Amsterdam* (1998) won the Man Booker Prize. *Atonement* (2001) was made into an Oscar-winning film and gathered a lot of praise. In 2011, he was awarded the Jerusalem Prize. He is a prolific writer with almost 30 written works. Till now Ian has been nominated for the Man Booker prize 6 times, and also lots of other awards in the field of literature.

As a metafiction novel, *Atonement* concerns the understanding and responding to the need for personal atonement. In 2007, this novel was included in the list of "100 greatest English language novels since 1923".

﹨ Plot

Briony Tallis, a 13-year-old girl, is from a wealthy English family. She loves writing plays and always indulges in her imagination. She witnesses a superficial tension between her elder sister, Cecilia, and Robbie Turner, the housekeeper's son. Robbie writes a letter to Cecilia, but mistakenly asks Briony to send the erotic draft letter to Cecilia. Briony secretly reads the letter and feels disgusted and jealous. Soon there comes up a case of rape, and Briony tells others that Robbie is the rapist. Everyone believes her words except Cecilia and Robbie's mother. Robbie is arrested and put into prison, while Cecilia breaks her contact with her family and becomes a nurse during World War II.

Robbie joins the army to get released from prison. Briony, now 18, gives up Cambridge University and also becomes a nurse. She tries to contact her sister and Robbie, but Cecillia can't forgive her while Robbie demands her to tell the truth in public. However, Briony's apology is weak and can never change anything because she knows the real rapist and the raped have just got married. However, in the final part of the book, writer Briony comes out and confesses that the ending of the book is all fictional. Cecilia and Robbie were never reunited. Robbie died during the war and Cecilia died as a victim of bomb during the Blitz.

Suggested Movie Version

Atonement was directed by Joe Wright in 2007. The roles of Cecilia and Robbie are played by British actress Keira Knightley and Scottish actor James McAvoy Robbie, while the role of Briony is played by American young actress Saoirse Ronan. It is filmed in England and Universal Studios manages the worldwide distribution. Ronan was nominated for an Oscar Best Supporting Actress. Also the film won Best Original Score at the 80th Academy Awards and the Golden Globe Award for Best Motion Picture-Drama. The actress Keira Knightley had co-operations with Director Joe Wright twice and was praised for her "naturalism" in the performance. To 12-year-old Saoirse Ronan, the film was her first casting experience which received a lot of appreciation. While Ronan played the role of Briony at the age of 13, English actresses Romola Garai and Vanessa Redgrave played the roles of Briony at the age of 18 and 77 respectively.

Important Quotations

LONDON, 1999

... Now it is five in the morning and I am still at the writing desk, thinking over my strange two days. It's true about the old not needing sleep—at least, not in the night. I still have so much to consider, and soon, within the year perhaps, I'll have far less of a mind to do it with. I've been thinking about my last novel, the one that should have been my first. The earliest version, January 1940, the latest, March 1999, and in between, half a dozen different drafts. The second draft, June 1947, the third... who cares to know? My fifty-nine-year assignment is over. There was our crime—Lola's, Marshall's, mine—and from the second version onward, I set out to describe it. I've regarded it as my duty to disguise nothing—the names, the places, the exact circumstances—I put it all there as a matter of historical record. But as a matter of legal reality, so various editors have told me over the years, my forensic memoir could never be published while my fellow criminals were alive. You may only libel yourself and the dead. The Marshalls have been active about the courts since the late forties, defending their good names with a most expensive ferocity. They could ruin a publishing house with ease from their current accounts. One might almost think they had something to hide. Think, yes, but not write. The obvious suggestions have been made— displace, transmute, dissemble. Bring down the fogs of the imagination! What are novelists for? Go just so far as is necessary, set up camp inches beyond the reach, the fingertips of the law. But no one knows these precise distances until a judgment is handed down. To be safe, one would have to be bland and obscure. I know I cannot publish until they are dead. And as of this morning,

I accept that will not be until I am. No good, just one of them going. Even with Lord Marshall's bone-shrunk mug on the obituary pages at last, my cousin from the north would not tolerate an accusation of criminal conspiracy.

There was a crime. But there were also the lovers. Lovers and their happy ends have been on my mind all night long. As into the sunset we sail. An unhappy inversion. It occurs to me that I have not traveled so very far after all, since I wrote my little play. Or rather, I've made a huge digression and doubled back to my starting place. It is only in this last version that my lovers end well, standing side by side on a South London pavement as I walk away. All the preceding drafts were pitiless. But now I can no longer think what purpose would be served if, say, I tried to persuade my reader, by direct or indirect means, that Robbie Turner died of septicemia at Bray Dunes on 1 June 1940, or that Cecilia was killed in September of the same year by the bomb that destroyed Balham Underground station. That I never saw them in that year. That my walk across London ended at the church on Clapham Common, and that a cowardly Briony limped back to the hospital, unable to confront her recently bereaved sister. That the letters the lovers wrote are in the archives of the War Museum. How could that constitute an ending? What sense or hope or satisfaction could a reader draw from such an account? Who would want to believe that they never met again, never fulfilled their love? Who would want to believe that, except in the service of the bleakest realism? I couldn't do it to them. I'm too old, too frightened, too much in love with the shred of life I have remaining. I face an incoming tide of forgetting, and then oblivion. I no longer possess the courage of my pessimism. When I am dead, and the Marshalls are dead, and the novel is finally published, we will only exist as my inventions. Briony will be as much of a fantasy as the lovers who shared a bed in Balham and enraged their landlady. No one will care what events and which individuals were misrepresented to make a novel. I know there's always a certain kind of reader who will be compelled to ask, But what really happened? The answer is simple: the lovers survive and flourish. As long as there is a single copy, a solitary typescript of my final draft, then my spontaneous, fortuitous sister and her medical prince survive to love.

The problem these fifty-nine years has been this: how can a novelist achieve atonement when, with her absolute power of deciding outcomes, she is also God? There is no one, no entity or higher form that she can appeal to, or be reconciled with, or that can forgive her. There is nothing outside her. In her imagination she has set the limits and the terms. No atonement for God, or novelists, even if they are atheists. It was always an impossible task, and that was precisely the point. The attempt was all.

I've been standing at the window, feeling waves of tiredness beat the remaining strength from my body. The floor seems to be undulating beneath my feet. I've been watching the first gray light bring into view the park and the bridges over the vanished lake. And the long narrow driveway down which they drove Robbie away, into the whiteness. I like to think that it isn't weakness or evasion, but a final act of kindness, a stand against oblivion and despair, to let my lovers live and to unite them at the end. I gave them happiness, but I was not so self-serving as to let them forgive me. Not quite, not yet. If I had the power to conjure them at my birthday celebration… Robbie and Cecilia, still alive, still in love, sitting side by side in the library, smiling at The Trials of Arabella? It's not impossible.

But now I must sleep.

Quoted from

http://www.en8848.com.cn/fiction/Fiction/Gerneral/59136_29.html.

Clip of the Movie

The part when Robbie, Cecillia and Briony met years later.

Topics for Discussion

1. What would happen if Robbie gave the formal letter, rather than the draft, to Briony? Would Briony still make the same mistake?

2. How would you like to describe young Briony? How does her character affect the plot?

3. Why did the author, Ian McEwan, write this novel? Is this novel some indicator of social issues? Or is it some reflection of his personal experience?

Part Two

美国文学

Chapter 11　Hawthorne: *The Scarlet Letter*

＼ Context

In writing *The Scarlet Letter*, Hawthorne was creating a form of fiction he called the psychological romance, and woven throughout his novel are elements of Gothic literature. What he created would later be followed by other romances, but never would they attain the number of readers or the critical acclaim of *The Scarlet Letter*. Hawthorne began *The Scarlet Letter* in September, 1849, and finished it, amazingly, in February, 1850. Its publication made his literary reputation and temporarily eased some of his financial burdens. This novel was the culmination of Hawthorne's own reading, study, and experimentation with themes about the subjects of Puritans, sin, guilt, and the human conflict between emotions and intellect. Since its first publishing in March of 1850, *The Scarlet Letter* has never been out of print. Even today, Hawthorne's romance is one of the best-selling books in the market. Perhaps *The Scarlet Letter* is so popular, generation after generation, because its beauty lies in the layers of meaning and the uncertainties and ambiguities of the symbols and characters. Each generation can interpret it and see relevance in its subtle meanings and appreciate the genius lying behind what many critics call "the perfect book". In *The Scarlet Letter*, the reader should be prepared to meet the real and the unreal, the actual and the imaginary, the probable and the improbable, all seen in the moonlight with the warmer light of a coal fire changing their hues.

＼ Plot

In June 1642, in the Puritan town of Boston, a crowd of people gather to witness an official punishment. A young woman, Hester Prynne, has been found guilty of adultery and must wear a scarlet A on her dress as a sign of shame. Furthermore, she must stand on the scaffold for three hours, exposed to public humiliation. As Hester approaches the scaffold, many of the women in the crowd are angered by her beauty and quiet dignity. When demanded and cajoled to name the father of her child, Hester refuses. As Hester looks out over the crowd, she notices a small, misshapen man and recognizes him as her long-lost husband, who has been presumed lost at sea. When her husband sees Hester's shame, he asks a man in the crowd about her and is told the story of his wife's adultery. He angrily exclaims that the child's father, the partner in the adulterous act, should also be punished and vows to find the man. He chooses a new name—Roger Chillingworth—to aid him in his plan. Reverend John Wilson and the minister of her church, Arthur Dimmesdale, question Hester, but she refuses to name her lover. After she returns to her prison cell, the jailer brings in Roger Chillingworth, a physician, to calm Hester and her child with his roots and herbs. Dismissing the jailer, Chillingworth first treats Pearl, Hester's baby, and then demands to know the name of the child's father. When Hester refuses, he insists that she never reveal that he is her husband. If she ever does so, he warns her, he will destroy the child's father. Hester agrees to Chillingworth's terms even though she suspects she will regret it. Following her release from prison, Hester settles in a cottage at the edge of town and earns a meager living with her needlework. She lives a quiet, somber life with her daughter, Pearl. She is troubled by her daughter's unusual character. As an infant, Pearl is fascinated by the scarlet A. As she grows older, Pearl becomes capricious and unruly. Her conduct starts rumors, and, not surprisingly, the church members suggest Pearl be taken away from Hester. Hester, hearing the rumors that she may lose Pearl, goes to speak to Governor Bellingham. With him are Reverends Wilson and Dimmesdale. When Wilson questions Pearl about her catechism, she refuses to answer, even though she knows the correct response, thus jeopardizing her guardianship. Hester appeals to Reverend Dimmesdale in desperation, and the minister persuades the governor to let Pearl remain in Hester's care. Because Reverend Dimmesdale's health has begun to fail, the townspeople are happy to have Chillingworth, a newly arrived physician, take up lodgings with their beloved minister. Being in such close contact with Dimmesdale, Chillingworth begins to suspect that the minister's illness is the result of some unconfessed guilt. He applies psychological pressure to the minister because he suspects Dimmesdale to be Pearl's father. One evening, pulling the sleeping Dimmesdale's vestment aside, Chillingworth sees something startling on the sleeping minister's pale chest: a scarlet A. Tormented by his guilty conscience, Dimmesdale goes to the square where Hester was punished years earlier. Climbing the scaffold, he sees Hester and Pearl and calls to them to join him. He admits his guilt to them but cannot find the courage to do so publicly. Suddenly Dimmesdale sees a meteor forming what appears to be a gigantic A in the sky; simultaneously, Pearl points toward the shadowy figure of Roger Chillingworth. Hester, shocked by Dimmesdale's deterioration, decides to obtain a release from her vow of silence to her husband. In her discussion of this with Chillingworth, she tells him his obsession with revenge must be stopped in order to save his own soul. Several days later, Hester meets Dimmesdale in the forest, where she removes the scarlet letter from her dress and identifies her husband and his desire for revenge. In this conversation, she convinces Dimmesdale to leave Boston in secret on a ship to Europe where they can start life anew. Renewed by this plan, the minister seems to gain new energy. Pearl, however, refuses to acknowledge either of them until Hester replaces her symbol of shame on her dress. Returning to town, Dimmesdale loses heart in their plan: He has become a changed man and knows he is dying. Meanwhile, Hester is informed by the captain of the ship on which she arranged passage that Roger Chillingworth will also be a passenger. On Election Day, Dimmesdale gives what is declared to be one of his most inspired sermons. But as the procession leaves the church, Dimmesdale stumbles and almost falls. Seeing Hester and Pearl in the crowd watching the parade, he climbs upon the scaffold and confesses his sin, dying in Hester's arms. Later, witnesses swear that they saw a stigmata in the form of a scarlet A upon his chest. Chillingworth, losing his revenge, dies shortly thereafter and leaves Pearl a great deal of money, enabling her to go to Europe with her mother and make a wealthy marriage. Several years later, Hester returns to Boston, resumes wearing the scarlet letter, and becomes a person to whom other women turn for solace. When she dies, she is buried near the grave of Dimmesdale, and they share a simple slate tombstone with the inscription "On a field, sable, the letter A gules".

＼ Suggested Movie Version

The Scarlet Letter is a 1995 American film adaptation of the Nathaniel Hawthorne novel of the same name. It was directed by Roland Joffé and stars Demi Moore, Gary Oldman, and Robert Duvall. This version was "freely adapted" from Hawthorne and deviated from the original story. It was nominated for seven Golden Raspberry Awards at the 1995 ceremony, winning "Worst Remake or Sequel".

The film drew scoffing and hostile reviews. Review aggregator Rotten Tomatoes gave the film a 14% approval rating, based on 35 reviews. It won the Golden Raspberry Award for "Worst Remake or Sequel" and was nominated for Worst Actress, Worst Director, Worst Picture, Worst Screen Couple, Worst Screenplay and Worst Supporting Actor. It grossed $10.3 million against a production budget of $50 million.

In response to the negative criticism, and to the new ending, Demi Moore said that the story the filmmakers were trying to tell differed out of necessity with that of the book, which she said was "very dense and not cinematic". She noted the original story might be better suited to a miniseries on television, and that the story presented in this film needed a different ending, one that did not lose "the ultimate message of Hester Prynne" that its makers were trying to convey.

＼ Important Quotations

Introduction to *The Scarlet Letter*

Doubtless, however, either of these stern and black-browed Puritans would have thought it quite a sufficient retribution for his sins that, after so long a lapse of years, the old trunk of the family tree, with so much venerable moss upon it, should have borne, as its topmost bough, an idler like myself. No aim that I have ever cherished would they recognise as laudable; no success of mine—if my life, beyond its domestic scope, had ever been brightened by success—would they deem otherwise than worthless, if not positively disgraceful. "What is he?" murmurs one grey shadow of my forefathers to the other. "A writer of story books! What kind of business in life— what mode of glorifying God, or being serviceable to mankind in his day and generation—may that be? Why, the degenerate fellow might as well have been a fiddler!" Such are the compliments bandied between my great grandsires and myself, across the gulf of time and yet, let them scorn me as they will, strong traits of their nature have intertwined themselves with mine.

Planted deep, in the town's earliest infancy and childhood, by these two earnest and energetic men, the race has ever since subsisted here; always, too, in respectability; never, so far as I have known, disgraced by a single unworthy member; but seldom or never, on the other hand, after the first two generations, performing any memorable deed, or so much as putting forward a claim to public notice. Gradually, they have sunk almost out of sight; as old houses, here and there about the streets, get covered half-way to the eaves by the accumulation of new soil. From father to son, for above a hundred years, they followed the sea; a grey-headed shipmaster, in each generation, retiring from the quarter-deck to the homestead, while a boy of fourteen took the hereditary place before the mast, confronting the salt spray and the gale which had blustered against his sire and grandsire. The boy, also in due time, passed from the forecastle to the cabin, spent a tempestuous manhood, and returned from his world-wanderings, to grow old, and die, and mingle his dust with the natal earth. This long connexion of a family with one spot, as its place of birth and burial, creates a kindred between the human being and the locality, quite independent of any charm in the scenery or moral circumstances that surround him. It is not love but instinct. The new inhabitant—who came himself from a foreign land, or whose father or grandfather came—has little claim to be called a Salemite; he has no conception of the oyster—like tenacity with which an old settler, over whom his third century is creeping, clings to the spot where his successive generations have been embedded. It is no matter that the place is joyless for him; that he is weary of the old wooden houses, the mud and dust, the dead level of site and sentiment, the chill east wind, and the chillest of social atmospheres; —all these, and whatever faults besides he may see or imagine, are nothing to the purpose. The spell survives, and just as powerfully as if the natal spot were an earthly paradise. So has it been in my case. I felt it almost as a destiny to make Salem my home; so that the mould of features and cast of character which had all along been familiar here— ever, as one representative of the race lay down in the grave, another assuming, as it were, his sentry-march along the main street—might still in my little day be seen and recognised in the old town. Nevertheless, this very sentiment is an evidence that the connexion, which has become an unhealthy one, should at least be severed. Human nature will not flourish, any more than a potato, if it be planted and re-planted, for too long a series of generations, in the same worn-out soil. My children have had other birth-places, and, so far as their fortunes may be within my control, shall strike their roots into accustomed earth.

Chapter 16

"Mother," said little Pearl, "the sunshine does not love you. It runs away and hides itself, because it is afraid of something on your bosom. Now, see! There it is, playing a good way off.

Stand you here, and let me run and catch it. I am but a child. It will not flee from me—for I wear nothing on my bosom yet!"

"Nor ever will, my child, I hope," said Hester.

"And why not, mother?" asked Pearl, stopping short, just at the beginning of her race. "Will not it come of its own accord when I am a woman grown?"

"Run away, child," answered her mother, "and catch the sunshine. It will soon be gone."

Pearl set forth at a great pace, and as Hester smiled to perceive, did actually catch the sunshine, and stood laughing in the midst of it, all brightened by its splendour, and scintillating with the vivacity excited by rapid motion. The light lingered about the lonely child, as if glad of such a playmate, until her mother had drawn almost nigh enough to step into the magic circle too.

"It will go now," said Pearl, shaking her head.

"See!" answered Hester, smiling; "now I can stretch out my hand and grasp some of it."

As she attempted to do so, the sunshine vanished; or, to judge from the bright expression that was dancing on Pearl's features, her mother could have fancied that the child had absorbed it into herself, and would give it forth again, with a gleam about her path, as they should plunge into some gloomier shade. There was no other attribute that so much impressed her with a sense of new and untransmitted vigour in Pearl's nature, as this never failing vivacity of spirits: she had not the disease of sadness, which almost all children, in these latter days, inherit, with the scrofula, from the troubles of their ancestors. Perhaps this, too, was a disease, and but the reflex of the wild energy with which Hester had fought against her sorrows before Pearl's birth. It was certainly a doubtful charm, imparting a hard, metallic lustre to the child's character. She wanted—what some people want throughout life—a grief that should deeply touch her, and thus humanise and make her capable of sympathy. But there was time enough yet for little Pearl.

Conclusion

But there was a more real life for Hester Prynne, here, in New England, that in that unknown region where Pearl had found a home. Here had been her sin; here, her sorrow; and here was yet to be her penitence. She had returned, therefore, and resumed of her own free will, for not the sternest magistrate of that iron period would have imposed it—resumed the symbol of which we have related so dark a tale. Never afterwards did it quit her bosom. But, in the lapse of the toilsome, thoughtful, and self-devoted years that made up Hester's life, the scarlet letter ceased to be a stigma which attracted the world's scorn and bitterness, and became a type of something to be sorrowed over, and looked upon with awe, yet with reverence too. And, as Hester Prynne had no selfish ends, nor lived in any measure for her own profit and enjoyment, people brought all their sorrows and perplexities, and besought her counsel, as one who had herself gone through a mighty trouble. Women, more especially—in the continually recurring trials of wounded, wasted, wronged, misplaced, or erring and sinful passion—or with the dreary burden of a heart unyielded, because unvalued and unsought came to Hester's cottage, demanding why they were so wretched, and what the remedy! Hester comforted and counselled them, as best she might. She assured them, too, of her firm belief that, at some brighter period, when the world should have grown ripe for it, in Heaven's own time, a new truth would be revealed, in order to establish the whole relation between man and woman on a surer ground of mutual happiness. Earlier in life, Hester had vainly imagined that she herself might be the destined prophetess, but had long since recognised the impossibility that any mission of divine and mysterious truth should be confided to a woman stained with sin, bowed down with shame, or even burdened with a life-long sorrow. The angel and apostle of the coming revelation must be a woman, indeed, but lofty, pure, and beautiful, and wise; moreover, not through dusky grief, but the ethereal medium of joy; and showing how sacred love should make us happy, by the truest test of a life successful to such an end.

So said Hester Prynne, and glanced her sad eyes downward at the scarlet letter. And, after many, many years, a new grave was delved, near an old and sunken one, in that burial-ground beside which King's Chapel has since been built. It was near that old and sunken grave, yet with a space between, as if the dust of the two sleepers had no right to mingle. Yet one tomb-stone served for both. All around, there were monuments carved with armorial bearings; and on this simple slab of slate—as the curious investigator may still discern, and perplex himself with the purport—there appeared the semblance of an engraved escutcheon. It bore a device, a herald's wording of which may serve for a motto and brief description of our now concluded legend; so sombre is it, and relieved only by one ever-glowing point of light gloomier than the shadow:—

"ON A FIELD, SABLE, THE LETTER A, GULES"

Quoted from

http://novel.tingroom.com/jingdian/67/.

Clip of the Movie

The part when Reverend Dimmesdale confessed his guilt and sin, and died.

Topics for Discussion

1. What are the differences between the ending of the movie and that of the book? Do you think these differences are acceptable?

2. The original work has many questions unsolved. For example, why, where, and how, exactly, did Hester and Dimmesdale get together? How did Hester manage on her

own, without either child-support or day-care? What happened to Chillingworth during his long captivity? And the movie tried to provide the audience with some explainable context from the film-making's point of view. To its surprise, it was reviewed as the worst adaptation. What are the possible reasons?

Chapter 12　Wharton: *The Age of Innocence*

⟍ Context

Edith Wharton (1862—1937) was a Pulitzer Prize winning American novelist. She was always in the pool of Nobel Prize in Literature, namely in 1927, 1928 and 1930. Wharton was born at an America's privileged class and well acquainted with many celebrated literary and public figures including Henry James and Theodore Roosevelt. Of all her novels and stories, Wharton held the features of humor and incisiveness with social and psychological insight.

The Age of Innocence is Wharton's twelfth novel, which made her the first woman to win the Pulitzer Prize for Fiction in 1921, or "First Lady of Letters". The setting of the story is of the upper-class in New York City in the 1870s, "the Gilded Age". In Wharton's term, "Old New York" refers to the rich and elite class at the top of social hierarchy in the 1870s America. As it shows in *The Age of Innocence*, Old New York set social code for its members in all aspects. Once the code was breached they were punished with exquisite politeness. So, *The Age of Innocence* is Wharton's connection of her early luxurious life with the astounding social changes, comparing her own past with the new age.

Edith Wharton put the conflict between individuals and the whole class as the central theme in *The Age of Innocence*. Also as a writer, Wharton was criticized by her own class for having bohemian style of life, into which artists and writers always fall.

⟍ Plot

Newland Archer is a rich young lawyer with engagement to May Welland, a seemingly innocent young girl of Old New York Society. May's cousin, Countess Ellen Olenska returns to America after her separation from her husband. Rumors come around of Ellen's adultery as well as her carefree behaviors. However, because of the family stand, Archer and May have to befriend her. Meanwhile, Ellen's unconventional views greatly attract Archer. He begins to fall in love with her and feel disappointed with May who lacks sense of self and follows rules of her class. Stunned by this fact, Archer hurries to speed up his wedding with May while he admits his love with Ellen. After the wedding, the couple settle down in New York. News comes that Ellen's husband wants Ellen to go back to Europe, which Ellen refuses. However, Archer and Ellen can't help their love for each other. One day Ellen suddenly announces her return to Europe. In the farewell party to Ellen, May tells Archer that she is pregnant and she has told Ellen about it two weeks earlier.

Since then, Archer spends 25 years with May during which they have 3 children and finally May is dead from pneumonia. Archer's son travels to France with Archer and plans to visit Ellen's apartment. However, at the last minute Archer stops and sends his son alone to Ellen, content with his memories of the past.

＼ Suggested Movie Version

The Age of Innocence (1993) was directed by Martin Scorses, the American director, producer and screenwriter. It won the Academy Award for Best Costume Design and was nominated for Best Supporting Actress, Best Art Direction and others. It also won the Golden Globe Award for Best Supporting Actress.

English actor Daniel Day-Lewis played the role of Newland Archer. Day-Lewis is one of only three male actors who has ever won three Oscars, and also got a knighthood at Buckingham Palace for his excellence in drama in 2014. The role of Ellen Olenska was played by American actress Michelle M. Pfeiffer. Pfeiffer is among the most talented actresses in Hollywood, well-known for her versatility. The role of Ellen in *The Age of Innocence* made her win Elvira Notari Prize at the Venice Film Festival. Another American actress Winona Ryder took the role of May. She is one of the most iconic actresses of the 1990s. Her role of May received critical praise from the public.

Though this film is not commercially successful, it won positive reviews from the public. This film version is the most recent till now.

＼ Important Quotations

Chapter 24

She had grown tired of what people called "society"; New York was kind, it was almost oppressively hospitable; she should never forget the way in which it had welcomed her back; but after the first flush of novelty she had found herself, as she phrased it, too "different" to care for the things it cared about—and so she had decided to try Washington, where one was supposed to meet more varieties of people and of opinion. And on the whole she should probably settle down in Washington, and make a home there for poor Medora, who had worn out the patience of all her other relations just at the time when she most needed looking after and protecting from matrimonial perils.

...

"Ah, it's what I've always told you; you don't like us. And you like Beaufort because he's so unlike us." He looked about the bare room and out at the bare beach and the row of stark white village houses strung along the shore. "We're damnably dull. We've no character, no colour, no variety. —I wonder," he broke out, "why you don't go back?"

Her eyes darkened, and he expected an indignant rejoinder. But she sat silent, as if thinking over what he had said, and he grew frightened lest she should answer that she wondered too.

At length she said: "I believe it's because of you."

It was impossible to make the confession more dispassionately, or in a tone less encouraging to the vanity of the person addressed. Archer reddened to the temples, but dared not move or speak: it was as if her words had been some rare butterfly that the least motion might drive off on startled wings, but that might gather a flock about it if it were left undisturbed.

"At least," she continued, "it was you who made me understand that under the dullness there are things so fine and sensitive and delicate that even those I most cared for in my other life look cheap in comparison. I don't know how to explain myself"—she drew together her troubled brows— "but it seems as if I'd never before understood with how much that is hard and shabby and base the most exquisite pleasures may be paid."

"Exquisite pleasures—it's something to have had them!" he felt like retorting; but the appeal in her eyes kept him silent.

"I want," she went on, "to be perfectly honest with you—and with myself. For a long time I've hoped this chance would come: that I might tell you how you've helped me, what you've made of me—"

Archer sat staring beneath frowning brows. He interrupted her with a laugh. "And what do you make out that you've made of me?"

She paled a little. "Of you?"

"Yes: for I'm of your making much more than you ever were of mine. I'm the man who married one woman because another one told him to."

Her paleness turned to a fugitive flush. "I thought— you promised—you were not to say such things today."

"Ah—how like a woman! None of you will ever see a bad business through!"

She lowered her voice. "IS it a bad business—for May?"

He stood in the window, drumming against the raised sash, and feeling in every fibre the wistful tenderness with which she had spoken her cousin's name.

"For that's the thing we've always got to think of—haven't we—by your own showing?" she insisted.

"My own showing?" he echoed, his blank eyes still on the sea.

"Or if not," she continued, pursuing her own thought with a painful application, "if it's not worth while to have given up, to have missed things, so that others may be saved from disillusionment and misery—then everything I came home for, everything that made my other life seem by contrast so bare and so poor because no one there took account of them—all these things are a sham or a dream—"

He turned around without moving from his place. "And in that case there's no reason on earth why you shouldn't go back?" he concluded for her.

Her eyes were clinging to him desperately. "Oh, is there no reason?"

"Not if you staked your all on the success of my marriage. My marriage," he said savagely, "isn't going to be a sight to keep you here." She made no answer, and he went on: "What's the use? You gave me my first glimpse of a real life, and at the same moment you asked me to go on with a sham one. It's beyond human enduring—that's all."

"Oh, don't say that; when I'm enduring it!" she burst out, her eyes filling.

Her arms had dropped along the table, and she sat with her face abandoned to his gaze as if in the recklessness of a desperate peril. The face exposed her as much as if it had been her whole person, with the soul behind it: Archer stood dumb, overwhelmed by what it suddenly told him.

"You too—oh, all this time, you too?"

For answer, she let the tears on her lids overflow and run slowly downward.

Half the width of the room was still between them, and neither made any show of moving. Archer was conscious of a curious indifference to her bodily presence: he would hardly have been aware of it if one of the hands she had flung out on the table had not drawn his gaze as on the occasion when, in the little Twenty-third Street house, he had kept his eye on it in order not to look at her face. Now his imagination spun about the hand as about the edge of a vortex; but still he made no effort to draw nearer. He had known the love that is fed on caresses and feeds them; but this passion that was closer than his bones was not to be superficially satisfied. His one terror was to do anything which might efface the sound and impression of her words; his one thought, that he should never again feel quite alone.

But after a moment the sense of waste and ruin overcame him. There they were, close together and safe and shut in; yet so chained to their separate destinies that they might as well have been half the world apart.

"What's the use—when you will go back?" he broke out, a great hopeless HOW ON EARTH CAN I KEEP YOU? crying out to her beneath his words.

She sat motionless, with lowered lids. "Oh—I shan't go yet!"

"Not yet? Some time, then? Some time that you already foresee?"

At that she raised her clearest eyes. "I promise you: not as long as you hold out. Not as long as we can look straight at each other like this."

He dropped into his chair. What her answer really said was: "If you lift a finger you'll drive me back: back to all the abominations you know of, and all the temptations you half guess." He understood it as clearly as if she had uttered the words, and the thought kept him anchored to his side of the table in a kind of moved and sacred submission.

"What a life for you!—" he groaned.

"Oh—as long as it's a part of yours."

"And mine a part of yours?"

Quoted from

http://www.online-literature.com/wharton/innocence/24/.

Clip of the Movie

The part when May told Archer that she was pregnant and that she has also told Ellen about it two weeks ago.

Topics for Discussion

1. Some readers think that Archer makes good choice to stay with May while others think that Archer should break away from May and choose Ellen. What will you choose if you were Archer, and why?

2. Wharton's novel is always dominated by the values and morals of upper class women. In what ways is the New York society of the novel a woman's world?

3. May is always pure, pretty and innocent. She behaves in good ways as a young girl and a wife. She succeeds in getting married to Archer and has a family with three children. Do you think she is innocent and happy? Why or why not?

Chapter 13　Alcott: *Little Women*

＼Context

Little Women is a novel by American author Louisa May Alcott, which was originally published in two volumes in 1868 and 1869. Alcott wrote the books rapidly within several months at the request of her publisher. The novel follows the lives of four sisters—Meg, Jo, Beth, and Amy March—detailing their passage from childhood to womanhood, and is loosely based on the author and her three sisters.

Little Women was an immediate commercial and critical success. Alcott quickly completed a second volume. It was also successful. The two volumes were issued in 1880 in a single work entitled *Little Women*. Although *Little Women* was a novel for girls, it differed notably from the current writings for children, especially girls. The novel addressed three major themes: "domesticity, work, and true love", all of them interdependent and each necessary to the achievement of its heroine's individual identity.

The book has been adapted for film twice as silent films, and four times with sound in 1933, 1949, 1978, and 1994. Four television series were made, including two in Britain in the 1950s and two anime series in Japan in the 1980s. A musical version opened on Broadway in 2005. An American opera version in 1998 has been performed internationally and filmed for broadcast on US television in 2001.

＼Plot

Four sisters live with their mother, facing Christmas without their father as the US Civil War is underway. The family is settled in a new neighborhood, living in genteel poverty after the father loses their money. Meg and Jo March, the elder sisters, both work outside the home for money to support the family. Meg teaches four children in a nearby family, while Jo aids her grand-aunt March, a wealthy widow whose strength is failing. Beth helps around the house, and Amy attends school. Their nearest neighbor is a wealthy man whose orphaned grandson lives with him. The sisters introduce themselves to the handsome shy boy, who is the age of Jo. Meg is the beautiful sister; Jo is the tomboy; Beth is the musician; and Amy is the charming artist with blond curls. The boy Laurie enjoys his neighbors, joining the family often in play and home theatrics written by Jo. His grandfather, Mr. Laurence, is charmed by Beth, and gives her the piano used by Laurie's dead sister.

Beth contracts scarlet fever after tending to a family where three children have died of it. Her poor condition forces her sisters and the Laurences to call Marmee back from Washington, where she has gone to tend her husband, who has contracted pneumonia. Beth recovers, but never fully.

Jo tends Beth in her illness. Amy, not yet exposed to scarlet fever, is sent to live with Aunt March, replacing Jo after Beth recovers. Jo has succeeded earning money with her writing. Meg spends two weeks with friends, where there are parties for the girls to dance with boys and improve social skills. Laurie is invited to one of the dances, as her friends mistake that Meg is in love with him. Meg is more interested in the young tutor for Laurie, John Brooke. Brooke travels to Washington to help Mr. March, staying there when Marmee comes back to tend Beth. While with both March parents, Brooke confesses his love for Meg. The parents agree, but suggest they are both too young to marry, as Meg is just seventeen. They agree to wait. In the interim, Brooke serves a year in the war, is wounded, returns home and finds work so he can get a house for their upcoming marriage. Laurie's need for a tutor ends, as he goes off to college. The war ends.

Meg and John marry and settle in the house, close to the March home. They learn how to live together, and soon have twins. Laurie graduates from college, putting in effort to do well in his last year, at Jo's prompting. Jo decides she needs a break, and spends six months with a friend of her mother in New York City, serving as governess for her two children. Amy goes on a European tour with her aunt, uncle and cousin. Jo returns home, where Laurie proposes marriage to her, and she turns him down. He is heartbroken; both he and his grandfather go to Europe. Beth's health has seriously deteriorated, as Jo sees on her return. She devotes herself to the care of her sister, until Beth dies. In Europe, Laurie encounters Amy, who is growing up. On news of Beth's death, the two meet for consolation, and their romance grows strong, as Amy learns how to manage him. They marry in Europe. The day they return home, Professor Bhaer shows up at March's home. He spends two weeks there, on the last day proposing marriage to Jo. Their marriage is deferred as Bhaer teaches at a college in the west. Aunt March dies, leaving her large home, Plumfield, to Jo. She and Bhaer marry, turning the house into a school for boys. They have two sons of their own, and Amy and Laurie have a daughter. In the fall at apple-picking time, Marmee's 60th birthday is celebrated at Jo's place, with her three daughters, their husbands, her husband, and her five grandchildren.

＼ Suggested Movie Version

This version of Louisa May Alcott's tender novel is considered to be among the best as it chronicles the lives of four sisters growing up in the mid nineteenth century. The story is set in New England during and immediately after the Civil War. The four March sisters Meg, Jo, Beth, and Amy are living alone with their mother Marmee. Their father has left to fight in the Union Army and their standard of living and social status has been greatly reduced. The story primarily focuses upon Jo, a budding writer of adventure and crime stories. As the seasons turn and years pass the girls grow up. Meg marries her former tutor Brooke, Beth is damaged by scarlet fever, and Jo spurns Laurie after he proposes. Marmee advises Jo to celebrate her independence and Jo moves to New York where she becomes a trashy novelist under the pen name "Joseph". In New York she meets Friedrich Bhaer, a German philosophy professor. She feels an instant connection to him. Meanwhile Amy is in Europe studying art when she encounters Laurie who has become a playboy. After a family tragedy and at the behest of her mentor the professor, Jo changes her writing style and becomes Louisa May Alcott.

＼ Important Quotations

Part 1

Everybody sniffed when they came to that part; Jo wasn't ashamed of the great tear that dropped off the end of her nose, and Amy never minded the rumpling of her curls as she hid her face on her mother's shoulder and sobbed out, 'I am a selfish pig! but I'll truly try to be better, so he mayn't be disappointed in me by and by.' 'We all will!' cried Meg. 'I think too much of my looks, and hate to work, but won't any more, if I can help it.' 'I'll try and be what he loves to call me, "a little woman," and not be rough and wild; but do my duty here instead of wanting to be somewhere else,' said Jo, thinking that keeping her temper at home was a much harder task than facing a rebel or two down South. Beth said nothing, but wiped away her tears with the blue army sock, and began to knit with all her might, losing no time in doing the duty that lay nearest her, while she resolved in her quiet little soul to be all that father hoped to find her when the year brought round the happy coming home. Mrs. March broke the silence that followed Jo's words, by saying in her cheery voice, 'Do you remember how you used to play *Pilgrim's Progress* when you were little things? Nothing delighted you more than to have me tie my piece-bags on your backs for burdens, give you hats and sticks, and rolls of paper, and let you travel through the house from the cellar, which was the City of Destruction, up, up, to the house-top, where you had all the lovely things you could collect to make a Celestial City.' 'What fun it was, especially going by the lions, fighting Apollyon, and passing through the Valley where the hobgoblins were,' said Jo. 'I liked the place where the bundles fell off and tumbled down stairs,' said Meg. 'My favorite part was when we came out on the flat roof where our flowers and arbors, and pretty things were, and all stood and sung for joy up there in the sunshine,' said Beth, smiling, as if that pleasant moment had come back to her. 'I don't remember much about it, except that I was afraid of the cellar and the dark entry, and always liked the cake and milk we had up at the top. If I wasn't too old for such things, I'd rather like to play it over again,' said Amy, who began to talk of renouncing childish things at the mature age of twelve. 'We never are too old for this, my dear, because it is a play we are playing all the time in one way or another. Our burdens are here, our road is before us, and the longing for goodness and happiness is the guide that leads us through many troubles and mistakes to the peace which is a true Celestial City. Now, my little pilgrims, suppose you begin again, not in play, but in earnest, and see how far on you can get before father comes home.' 'Really, mother? where are our bundles?' asked Amy, who was a very literal young lady. 'Each of you told what your burden was just now, except Beth; I rather think she hasn't got any,' said her mother. 'Yes, I have; mine is dishes and dusters, and envying girls with nice pianos, and being afraid of people.' Beth's bundle was such a funny one that everybody wanted to laugh; but nobody did, for it would have hurt her feelings very much. 'Let us do it,' said Meg, thoughtfully. 'It is only another name for trying to be good, and the story may help us; for though we do want to be good, it's hard work, and we forget, and don't do our best.' 'We were in the Slough of Despond to-night, and mother came and pulled us out as Help did in the book. We ought to have our roll of directions, like Christian. What shall we do about that?' asked Jo, delighted with the fancy which lent a little romance to the very dull task of doing her duty. 'Look under your pillows, Christmas morning, and you will find your guide-book,' replied Mrs March. They talked over the new plan while old Hannah cleared the table; then out came the four little workbaskets, and the needles flew as the girls made sheets for Aunt March. It was uninteresting sewing, but to-night no one grumbled. They adopted Jo's plan of dividing the long seams into four parts, and calling the quarters Europe, Asia, Africa and America, and in that way got on capitally, especially when they talked about the different countries as they stitched their way through them. At nine they stopped work, and sung, as usual, before they went to bed. No one but Beth could get much music out of the old piano; but she had a way of softly touching the yellow keys, and making a pleasant accompaniment to the simple songs they sung. Meg had a voice like a flute, and she and her mother led the little choir. Amy chirped like a cricket, and Jo wandered through the airs at her own sweet will, always coming out at the wrong place with a crook or a quaver that spoilt the most pensive tune. They had always done this from the time they could lisp 'Crinkle, crinkle, 'ittle 'tar,' and it had become a household custom, for the mother was a born singer. The first sound in the morning was her voice, as she went about the house singing like a lark; and the last sound at night was the same cheery sound, for the girls never grew too old for that familiar lullaby.

Part 47

During this ceremony the boys had mysteriously disappeared; and, when Mrs. March had tried to thank her children, and broken down, while Teddy wiped her eyes on his pinafore, the Professor suddenly began to sing. Then, from above him, voice after voice took up the words, and from tree to tree echoed the music of the unseen choir, as the boys sung, with all their hearts, the little song Jo had written, Laurie set to music, and the Professor trained his lads to give with the best effect. This was something altogether new, and it proved a grand success, for Mrs. March couldn't get over her surprise, and insisted on shaking hands with every one of the featherless birds, from tall Franz and Emil to the little quadroon, who had the sweetest voice of all. After this, the boys dispersed for a final lark, leaving Mrs. March and her daughters under the festival tree. 'I don't think I ever ought to call myself 'Unlucky Jo' again, when my greatest wish has been so beautifully gratified,' said Mrs. Bhaer, taking Teddy's little fist out of the milk pitcher, in which he was rapturously churning. 'And yet your life is very different from the one you pictured so long ago. Do you remember our castles in the air?' asked Amy, smiling as she watched Laurie and John playing cricket with the boys. 'Dear fellows! It does my heart good to see them forget business, and frolic for a day,' answered Jo, who now spoke in a maternal way of all mankind. 'Yes, I remember; but the life I wanted then seems selfish, lonely and cold to me now. I haven't given up the hope that I may write a good book yet, but I can wait, and I'm sure it will be all the better for such experiences and illustrations as these;' and Jo pointed from the lively lads in the distance to her father, leaning on the Professor's arm, as they walked to and fro in the sunshine, deep in one of the conversations which both enjoyed so much, and then to her mother, sitting enthroned among her daughters, with their children in her lap and at her feet, as if all found help and happiness in the face which never could grow old to them. 'My castle was the most nearly realized of all. I asked for splendid things, to be sure, but in my heart I knew I should be satisfied, if I had a little home, and John, and some dear children like these. I've got them all, thank God, and I am the happiest woman in the world;' and Meg laid her hand on her tall boy's head, with a face full of tender and devout content. 'My castle is very different from what I planned, but I would not alter it, though, like Jo, I don't relinquish all my artistic hopes, or confine myself to helping others fulfill their dreams of beauty. I've begun to model a figure of baby, and Laurie says it is the best thing I've ever done. I think so myself, and mean to do it in marble, so that whatever happens, I may at least keep the image of my little angel.' As Amy spoke, a great tear dropped on the golden hair of the sleeping child in her arms; for her one well-beloved daughter was a frail little creature, and the dread of losing her was the shadow over Amy's sunshine. This cross was doing much for both father and mother, for one love and sorrow bound them closely together. Amy's nature was growing sweeter, deeper and more tender; Laurie was growing more serious, strong and firm, and both were learning that beauty, youth, good fortune, even love itself, cannot keep care and pain, loss and sorrow, from the most blest; for—'Into each life some rain must fall, Some days must be dark, and sad, and dreary.' 'She is growing better, I am sure of it, my dear; don't despond, but hope, and keep happy,' said Mrs. March, as tender-hearted Daisy stooped from her knee, to lay her rosy cheek against her little cousin's pale one. 'I never ought to, while I have you to cheer me up, Marmee, and Laurie to take more than half of every burden,' replied Amy, warmly. 'He never lets me see his anxiety, but is so sweet and patient with me, so devoted to Beth, and such a stay and comfort to me always, that I can't love him enough. So, in spite of my one cross, I can say with Meg, "Thank God,

I'm a happy woman." 'There's no need for me to say it, for everyone can see that I'm far happier than I deserve,' added Jo, glancing from her good husband to her chubby children, tumbling on the grass beside her. 'Fritz is getting gray and stout, I'm growing as thin as a shadow, and am over thirty; we never shall be rich, and Plumfield may burn up any night, for that incorrigible Tommy Bangswill smoke sweetfern cigars under the bed-clothes, though he's set himself afire three times already. But in spite of these unromantic facts, I have nothing to complain of, and never was so jolly in my life. Excuse the remark, but living among boys, I can't help using their expressions now and then.' 'Yes, Jo, I think your harvest will be a good one,' began Mrs. March, frightening away a big black cricket, that was staring Teddy out of countenance. 'Not half so good as yours, mother. Here it is, and we never can thank you enough for the patient sowing and reaping you have done,' cried Jo, with the loving impetuosity which she never could outgrow. 'I hope there will be more wheat and fewer tares every year,' said Amy, softly. 'A large sheaf, but I know there's room in your heart for it, Marmee dear,' added Meg's tender voice. Touched to the heart, Mrs. March could only stretch out her arms, as if to gather children and grandchildren to herself, and say, with face and voice full of motherly love, gratitude, and humility,—'Oh, my girls, however long you may live, I never can wish you a greater happiness than this!'

Quoted from

http://novel.tingroom.com/jingdian/91/.

Clip of the Movie

The part when Mrs. March and her three daughters and five grandchildren gathered together in the end.

Topics for Discussion

1. What do you think of the movie focusing more on Jo? Why does it do so?

2. Why is *Little Women* helpful in understanding American history when it seems that it pays more attention to the family affairs?

Chapter 14　Hemingway: *The Old Man and the Sea*

Context

In April of 1936, Hemingway published an essay in *Esquire* magazine entitled "On the Blue Water: A Gulf Stream Letter", which contained a paragraph about an old man who went fishing alone in a skiff far out at sea, landed a huge marlin, and then lost much of it to sharks. As early as 1939, the year he moved to Cuba, Hemingway began planning an expansion of this kernel into a fully developed story that would become part of a larger volume. Early in 1951, Hemingway finally began writing *The Old Man and the Sea* at his home near Havana. Although *The Old Man and the Sea* takes place in September of 1950, it exists outside of many significant political events of the period. However, the novella does reflect a universal pattern of socioeconomic change familiar even today among developing nations. In rural Cuba of the 1930s and 1940s, the traditional fishing culture began shifting to the material progress of a fishing industry. In *The Old Man and the Sea*, Hemingway depicts Santiago as a dedicated fisherman whose craft is integral to his own identity, his code of behavior, and nature's order. On the other hand, Hemingway portrays the pragmatic younger fishermen as those who supply shark livers for the cod liver oil industry in the United States, use their profits to purchase motorized boats and other mechanized equipment, and approach their fishing strictly as a means to improve their material circumstances. The novella is truly universal in its consideration of the plight of an old man struggling against age, poverty, loneliness, and mortality to maintain his identity and dignity, reestablish his reputation in the community, and ensure for all time his relationship with those he loves and to whom he hopes to pass on everything he values most. Ultimately, Santiago's heroic struggle not only redeems himself but inspires and spiritually enriches those around him. He first published *The Old Man and the Sea* in its entirety in *Life* magazine in 1952. It gained immediate critical acclaim and earned Hemingway the Pulitzer Prize in 1953 and the American Academy of Arts and Letters' Award of Merit Medal for the Novel. It also contributed to his receiving the Nobel Prize for Literature in 1954.

Plot

For 84 days, the old fisherman Santiago has caught nothing. Alone, impoverished, and facing his own mortality, Santiago is now considered unlucky. So Manolin (Santiago's fishing partner until recently and the young man Santiago has taught since the age of five) has been constrained by his parents to fish in another more productive boat. Every evening, though, when Santiago again returns empty-handed, Manolin helps carry home the old man's equipment, keeps him company, and brings him food. On the morning of the 85th day, Santiago sets out before dawn on a three-day odyssey that takes him far out to sea. In search of an epic catch, he eventually does snag a marlin of epic proportions, enduring tremendous hardship to land the great fish. He straps the marlin along the length of his skiff and heads for home, hardly believing his own victory. Within an hour, a mako shark attacks the marlin, tearing away a great hunk of its flesh and mutilating Santiago's prize. Santiago fights the mako, enduring great suffering, and eventually kills it with his harpoon, which he loses in the struggle. The great tear in the marlin's flesh releases the fish's blood and scent into the water, attracting packs of shovel-nosed sharks. With whatever equipment remains on board, Santiago repeatedly fights off the packs of these scavengers, enduring exhaustion and great physical pain, even tearing something in his chest. Eventually, the sharks pick the marlin clean. Defeated, Santiago reaches shore and beaches the skiff. Alone in the dark, he looks back at the marlin's skeleton in the reflection from a street light and then stumbles home to his shack, falling face down onto his cot in exhaustion. The next morning, Manolin finds Santiago in his hut and cries over the old man's injuries. Manolin fetches coffee and hears from the other fisherman what he had already seen—that the marlin's skeleton lashed to the skiff is eighteen feet long, the greatest fish the village has known. Manolin sits with Santiago until he awakes and then gives the old man some coffee. The old man tells Manolin that he was beaten. But Manolin reassures him that the great fish didn't beat him and that they will fish together again, that luck doesn't matter, and that the old man still has much to teach him. That afternoon, some tourists see the marlin's skeleton waiting to go out with the tide and ask a waiter what it is. Trying to explain what happened to the marlin, the waiter replies, "Eshark." But the tourists misunderstand and assume that's what the skeleton is. Back in his shack, with Manolin sitting beside him, Santiago sleeps again and dreams of the young lions he had seen along the coast of Africa when he was a young man.

◥ Suggested Movie Version

The Old Man and the Sea is a Warnercolor 1958 film starring Spencer Tracy, in a portrayal for which he was nominated for a Best Actor Oscar. The screenplay was adapted by Peter Viertel from the novella of the same name by Ernest Hemingway, and the film was directed by John Sturges. Sturges called it "technically the sloppiest picture I have ever made".

Dimitri Tiomkin won the Academy Award for Best Original Score for his work on the film, one that was also nominated for Best Color Cinematography.

╲ Important Quotations

Chapter 1

He no longer dreamed of storms, nor of women, nor of great occurrences, nor of great fish, nor fights, nor contests of strength, nor of his wife. He only dreamed of places now and of the lions on the beach. They played like young cats in the dusk and he l oved them as he loved the boy. He never dreamed about the boy. He simply woke, looked out the open door at the moon and unrolled his trousers and put them on. He urinated outside the shack and then went up the road to wake the boy. He was shivering with t he morning cold. But he knew he would shiver himself warm and that soon he would be rowing.

Chapter 3

"The fish is my friend too," he said aloud. "I have never seen or heard of such a fish. But I must kill him. I am glad we do not have to try to kill the stars."Imagine if each day a man must try to kill the moon, he thought. The moon runs away. But imagine if a man each day should have to try to kill the sun? We were born lucky, he thought.

Then he was sorry for the great fish that had nothing to eat and his determination to kill him never relaxed in his sorrow for him. How many people will he feed, he thought. But are they worthy to eat him? No, of course not.

There is no one worthy of eating him from the manner of his behaviour and his great dignity.

I do not understand these things, he thought. But it is good that we do not have to try to kill the sun or the moon or the stars. It is enough to live on the sea and kill our true brothers.

Quoted from

http://novel.tingroom.com/shuangyu/453/.

Clip of the Movie

The part when Santiago sails back to his village on the fourth day.

Topics for Discussion

1. Sometimes when the original literary work is written within the setting that is impossible for film makers to recreate in the movies, and it will lead to a lack of imagination watching the movie and audience's disappointment towards the movie. If so, would you rather choose not to transfer the original work to the screen?

2. Should the movie script follow a classical literary work in almost every detail?

Chapter 15　Fitzgerald: *The Great Gatsby*

Context

The Great Gatsby, published in 1925, is hailed as one of the foremost pieces of American fiction of its time. It is a novel of triumph and tragedy, noted for the remarkable way its author captures a cross-section of American society. In *The Great Gatsby*, Fitzgerald holds a mirror up to the society of which he was a part. The initial success of the book was limited, although in the more than 75 years since it has come to be regarded as a classic piece of American short fiction. Today it provides readers with a portal to observe the life in the 1920s. Through his characters, he not only captures a snapshot of middle- and upperclass American life in the 1920s, but also conveys a series of criticisms as well. Through the characterization in *The Great Gatsby*, Fitzgerald explores the human condition as it is reflected in a world characterized by social upheaval and uncertainty, a world with a direct underlying historical basis. The Jazz Age society so clearly shown in *The Great Gatsby* is, in effect, on a very dangerous course when people like Tom, Daisy, and Jordan are at the top of the ladder, working hard to ensure no one else climbs as highly as they do. Through Gatsby, Fitzgerald demonstrates the enterprising Jazz Ager, someone who has worked hard and profited from listening and responding to the demands of the society. Fitzgerald's story, although a fiction, is informed by reality, helping to make it one of the most treasured pieces of early twentieth century American fiction.

Plot

The Great Gatsby is a story told by Nick Carraway, who was once Gatsby's neighbor, and he tells the story sometime after 1922, when the incidents that fill the book take place. As the story opens, Nick has just moved from the Midwest to West Egg, Long Island, seeking his fortune as a bond salesman. Shortly after his arrival, Nick travels across the Sound to the more fashionable East Egg to visit his cousin Daisy Buchanan and her husband, Tom. There he meets professional golfer Jordan Baker. The Buchanans and Jordan Baker live privileged lives, contrasting sharply in sensibility and luxury with Nick's more modest and grounded lifestyle. When Nick returns home that evening, he notices his neighbor, Gatsby, mysteriously standing in the dark and stretching his arms toward the water, and a solitary green light across the Sound. One day, Nick is invited to accompany Tom, a blatant adulterer, to meet his mistress, Myrtle Wilson, a middle-class woman whose husband runs a modest garage and gas station in the valley of ashes. After the group meets and journeys into the city, Myrtle phones friends to come over, and they all spend the afternoon drinking at Myrtle and Tom's apartment. The afternoon is filled with drunken behavior and ends ominously with Myrtle and Tom fighting over Daisy, his wife. Nick turns his attention to his mysterious neighbor, who hosts weekly parties for the rich and fashionable. Upon Gatsby's invitation, Nick attends one of the extravagant gatherings. As the summer unfolds, Gatsby and Nick become friends, and Jordan and Nick begin to see each other on a regular basis. Nick and Gatsby journey into the city one day and there Nick meets Meyer Wolfsheim, one of Gatsby's associates and Gatsby's link to organized crime. On the same day, while having tea with Jordan Baker, Nick learns the amazing story that Gatsby told him the night of his party. Gatsby is in love with Daisy Buchanan. They met years earlier when he was in the army but could not be together because he did not yet have the means to support her. In the intervening years, Gatsby made his fortune, all with the goal of winning Daisy back. It has come time for Gatsby to meet Daisy again, face-to-face. The day of the meeting arrives. Nick's house is perfectly prepared. When the former lovers meet, their reunion is slightly nervous, but shortly, the two are once again comfortable with each other. As the afternoon progresses, the three move the party from Nick's house to Gatsby's, where he takes special delight in showing Daisy his meticulously decorated house and his impressive array of belongings. At this point, Nick again lapses into memory, relating the story of Jay Gatsby. Moving back to the present, we discover that Daisy and Tom will attend one of Gatsby's parties. Tom, of course, spends his time chasing women, while Daisy and Gatsby sneak over to Nick's yard for a moment's privacy while Nick, accomplice in the affair, keeps guard. After the Buchanans leave, Gatsby tells Nick of his secret desire: to recapture the past. As the summer unfolds, Gatsby and Daisy's affair begins to grow and they see each other regularly. On one fateful day, the hottest and most unbearable of the summer, Gatsby and Nick journey to East Egg to have lunch with the Buchanans and Jordan Baker. Oppressed by the heat, Daisy suggests they take solace in a trip to the city. No longer hiding her love for Gatsby, Daisy pays him special attention and Tom picks up on what's going on. As the party prepares to leave for the city, Tom fetches a bottle of whisky. Tom, Nick, and Jordan drive in Gatsby's car, while Gatsby and Daisy drive Tom's coupe. Low on gas, Tom stops Gatsby's car at Wilson's gas station, where he sees that Wilson is not well. Like Tom, who has just learned of Daisy's affair, Wilson has just learned of Myrtle's secret life, and it has made him physically sick. Wilson announces his plans to take Myrtle out West, much to Tom's dismay. Tom has lost a wife and a mistress all in a matter of an hour. Absorbed in his own fears, Tom hastily drives into the city. Gatsby wants Daisy to admit she's never loved Tom but that, instead, she has always loved him. When Daisy is unable to do this, Gatsby declares that Daisy is going to leave Tom. Tom, though, understands Daisy far better than Gatsby does and knows she won't leave him: his wealth and power, matured through generations of privilege, will triumph over Gatsby's newly found wealth. As Tom's car nears Wilson's garage, they can all see that some sort of accident has occurred. Pulling over to investigate, they learn that Myrtle Wilson, Tom's mistress, has been hit and killed by a passing car that never bothered to stop, and it appears to have been Gatsby's car. Tom, Jordan, and Nick continue home to East Egg. Later, Nick learns that Daisy, not Gatsby, was driving the car, although Gatsby confesses he will take all the blame. Later that morning, while at work, Nick is unable to concentrate. He plans to take an early train home and check on Gatsby. The action then switches back to Wilson, who, distraught over his wife's death, sneaks out and goes looking for the driver who killed Myrtle. Nick retraces Wilson's journey, which placed him, by early afternoon, at Gatsby's house. Wilson murders Gatsby and then turns the gun on himself. After Gatsby's death, Nick is left to help make arrangements for his burial. What is most perplexing, though, is that no one seems concerned with Gatsby's death. Daisy and Tom mysteriously leave on a trip, and all the people who so eagerly attended his parties refuse to become involved. Despite all his popularity during his lifetime, in his death, Gatsby is completely forgotten. Nick, completely disillusioned with what he has experienced in the East, prepares to head back to the Midwest. Nick, disgusted by the carelessness and cruel nature of Tom, Daisy, and those like them, leaves Tom, proud of his own integrity. On the last night before leaving, Nick goes to Gatsby's mansion, then to the shore where Gatsby once stood, arms outstretched toward the green light. The novel ends prophetically, with Nick noting how we are all a little like Gatsby, boats moving up a river, going forward but continually feeling the pull of the past.

＼ Suggested Movie Version

The Great Gatsby is a 2013 3D epic romantic drama film based on F. Scott Fitzgerald's 1925 novel of the same name. The film was co-written and directed by Baz Luhrmann, and starred Leonardo DiCaprio as Gatsby. The film follows the life and times of millionaire Jay Gatsby and his neighbour Nick, who recounts his encounter with Gatsby at the height of the Roaring Twenties. The film was originally going to be released to theaters on December 25, 2012, but was moved to May 10, 2013 to accommodate the film being shown in 3D.

While the film received mixed reviews from critics, who praised the performances but criticized the editing, soundtrack, and lack of loyalty to the book, audiences responded much more positively, and F. Scott Fitzgerald's granddaughter praised the film, stating "Scott would have been proud". As of 2014, it is Baz Luhrmann's highest grossing film, earning over $350 million worldwide. At the 86th Academy Awards, the film won in both of its nominated categories with the awards for Best Production Design and Best Costume Design.

＼ Important Quotations

Chapter 3

He smiled understandingly—much more than understandingly. It was one of those rare smiles with a quality of eternal reassurance in it, that you may come across four or five times in life. It faced—or seemed to face—the whole external world for an instant, and then concentrated on you with an irresistible prejudice in your favor. It understood you just so far as you wanted to be understood, believed in you as you would like to believe in yourself, and assured you that it had precisely the impression of you that, at your best, you hoped to convey. Precisely at that point it vanished—and I was looking at an elegant young rough-neck, a year or two over thirty, whose elaborate formality of speech just missed being absurd. Some time before he introduced himself I'd got a strong impression that he was picking his words with care.

Almost at the moment when Mr. Gatsby identified himself, a butler hurried toward him with the information that Chicago was calling him on the wire. He excused himself with a small bow that included each of us in turn.

"If you want anything just ask for it, old sport," he urged me. "Excuse me. I will rejoin you later."

When he was gone I turned immediately to Jordan—constrained to assure her of my surprise. I had expected that Mr. Gatsby would be a florid and corpulent person in his middle years.

"Who is he?" I demanded.

"Do you know?"

"He's just a man named Gatsby."

"Where is he from, I mean? And what does he do?"

"Now *you're* started on the subject," she answered with a wan smile. "Well, he told me once he was an Oxford man." A dim background started to take shape behind him, but at her next remark it faded away.

"However, I don't believe it."

"Why not?" "I don't know," she insisted, "I just don't think he went there."

Something in her tone reminded me of the other girl's "I think he killed a man," and had the effect of stimulating my curiosity. I would have accepted without question the information that Gatsby sprang from the swamps of Louisiana or from the lower East Side of New York. That was comprehensible. But young men didn't—at least in my provincial inexperience I believed they didn't—drift coolly out of nowhere and buy a palace on Long Island Sound.

"Anyhow, he gives large parties," said Jordan, changing the subject with an urbane distaste for the concrete. "And I like large parties. They're so intimate. At small parties there isn't any privacy."

There was the boom of a bass drum, and the voice of the orchestra leader rang out suddenly above the echolalia of the garden.

"Ladies and gentlemen," he cried. "At the request of Mr. Gatsby we are going to play for you Mr. Vladimir Tostoff's latest work, which attracted so much attention at Carnegie Hall last May. If you read the papers, you know there was a big sensation." He smiled with jovial condescension, and added: "Some sensation!" Whereupon everybody laughed.

"The piece is known," he concluded lustily, "as Vladimir Tostoff's *Jazz History of the World*."

The nature of Mr. Tostoff's composition eluded me, because just as it began my eyes fell on Gatsby, standing alone on the marble steps and looking from one group to another with approving eyes. His tanned skin was drawn attractively tight on his face and his short hair looked as though it were trimmed every day. I could see nothing sinister about him. I wondered if the fact that he was not drinking helped to set him off from his guests, for it seemed to me that he grew more correct as the fraternal hilarity increased. When the *Jazz History of the World* was over, girls were putting their heads on men's shoulders in a puppyish, convivial way, girls were swooning backward playfully into men's arms, even into groups, knowing that some one would arrest their falls—ut no one swooned backward on Gatsby, and no French bob touched Gatsby's shoulder, and no singing quartets were formed with Gatsby's head for one link.

Chapter 9

That's my Middle West—not the wheat or the prairies or the lost Swede towns, but the thrilling returning trains of my youth, and the street lamps and sleigh bells in the frosty dark and the shadows of holly wreaths thrown by lighted windows on the snow. I am part of that, a little solemn with the feel of those long winters, a little complacent from growing up in the Carraway house in a city where dwellings are still called through decades by a family's name. I see now that this has been a story of the West, after all—Tom and Gatsby, Daisy and Jordan and I, were all Westerners, and perhaps we possessed some deficiency in common which made us subtly unadaptable to Eastern life.

Even when the East excited me most, even when I was most keenly aware of its superiority to the bored, sprawling, swollen towns beyond the Ohio, with their interminable inquisitions which spared only the children and the very old—even then it had always for me a quality of distortion. West Egg, especially, still figures in my more fantastic dreams. I see it as a night scene by El Greco: a hundred houses, at once conventional and grotesque, crouching under a sullen, overhanging sky and a lustreless moon. In the foreground four solemn men in dress suits are walking along the sidewalk with a stretcher on which lies a drunken woman in a white evening dress. Her hand, which dangles over the side, sparkles cold with jewels. Gravely the men turn in at a house—the wrong house. But no one knows the woman's name, and no one cares.

After Gatsby's death the East was haunted for me like that, distorted beyond my eyes' power of correction. So when the blue smoke of brittle leaves was in the air and the wind blew the wet laundry stiff on the line I decided to come back home.

There was one thing to be done before I left, an awkward, unpleasant thing that perhaps had better have been let alone. But I wanted to leave things in order and not just trust that obliging and indifferent sea to sweep my refuse away. I saw Jordan Baker and talked over and around what had happened to us together, and what had happened afterward to me, and she lay perfectly still, listening, in a big chair.

She was dressed to play golf, and I remember thinking she looked like a good illustration, her chin raised a little jauntily, her hair the color of an autumn leaf, her face the same brown tint as the fingerless glove on her knee. When I had finished she told me without comment that she was engaged to another man. I doubted that, though there were several she could have married at a nod of her head, but I pretended to be surprised. For just a minute I wondered if I wasn't making a mistake, then I thought it all over again quickly and got up to say good-bye.

"Nevertheless you did throw me over," said Jordan suddenly. "You threw me over on the telephone. I don't give a damn about you now, but it was a new experience for me, and I felt a little dizzy for a while."

We shook hands.

"Oh, and do you remember."—she added—"a conversation we had once about driving a car?"

"Why—not exactly."

"You said a bad driver was only safe until she met another bad driver? Well, I met another bad driver, didn't I? I mean it was careless of me to make such a wrong guess. I thought you were rather an honest, straightforward person. I thought it was your secret pride."

"I'm thirty," I said. "I'm five years too old to lie to myself and call it honor."

She didn't answer. Angry, and half in love with her, and tremendously sorry, I turned away.

Chapter 9

Most of the big shore places were closed now and there were hardly any lights except the shadowy, moving glow of a ferryboat across the Sound. And as the moon rose higher the inessential houses began to melt away until gradually I became aware of the old island here that flowered once for Dutch sailors' eyes—a fresh, green breast of the new world. Its vanished trees, the trees that had made way for Gatsby's house, had once pandered in whispers to the last and greatest of all human dreams; for a transitory enchanted moment man must have held his breath in the presence of this continent, compelled into an aesthetic contemplation he neither understood nor desired, face to face for the last time in history with something commensurate to his capacity for wonder.

And as I sat there brooding on the old, unknown world, I thought of Gatsby's wonder when he first picked out the green light at the end of Daisy's dock. He had come a long way to this blue lawn, and his dream must have seemed so close that he could hardly fail to grasp it. He did not know that it was already behind him, somewhere back in that vast obscurity beyond the city, where the dark fields of the republic rolled on under the night.

Gatsby believed in the green light, the orgastic future that year by year recedes before us. It eluded us then, but that's no matter—to-morrow we will run faster, stretch out our arms farther... And one fine morning—

So we beat on, boats against the current, borne back ceaselessly into the past.

Quoted from

http://vdisk.weibo.com/s/dTrdZh8kfaNb.

Clip of the Movie

The part when Gatsby killed himself in the swimming pool at the end of the movie.

Topics for Discussion

1. *The Great Gatsby* received mixed reviews from critics. Among major critics, Joe Morgenstern of *The Wall Street Journal* felt the elaborate production designs were a misfire and what was "intractably wrong with the film is that there's no reality to heighten; it's a spectacle in search of a soul". It seems that the movie focuses more on the surface, including costumes, and music. Is the characterization, esp. thoughts, being neglected?

2. The ending of the movie and that of the original novel are quite different. Which one is more sensational and impressive?

Chapter 16 Steinbeck: *The Grapes of Wrath*

Context

The plot of Steinbeck's masterpiece is rooted in the historical and social events of 1930's, especially the environmental disaster that coined the Dust Bowl by an Oklahoma reporter in 1935. Drought had been a serious problem for the Great Plains region of the United States for many decades prior to the 1930s. Meanwhile, poor farming techniques of numerous sharecroppers had decimated the agricultural capacity of the land, the harsh cotton crops robbing soil of its nutrients. These two conditions combined to make it difficult for farmers to bring in a profitable crop. *The Grapes of Wrath* enjoyed immediate and widespread commercial success. Advanced sales of the novel shot it onto the national bestseller list where it was to stay throughout 1939 and 1940. Although mass circulation reviewers complained of its unconventional structure and downcast ending, the novel garnered a number of awards, including a Pulitzer Prize. However, not everyone was convinced of the novel's brilliance. In retrospect, it is probable that many people were ashamed by both the terrible dilemma of the migrant families and the inhumane treatment they received from society. In the years that followed, *The Grapes of Wrath* experienced a shift in critical reception. The passage of time had distanced the book from the volatile social and historical circumstances of its setting, allowing readers a clearer perspective of Steinbeck's work. At the time of its first appearance in 1939, the novel was considered, at best, an influential social tract. Following World War II, it became clear that if the novel were going to maintain its influential status, it would have to be considered not only for its social philosophies, but also for its artistic merits. Many respected literary critics began to seriously examine the literary elements of the novel. For the next three decades, indeed up to today, critics have delved into the work's artistic and conceptual traits, scrutinizing and debating its use of biblical allusions and symbolism, the effectiveness of its unconventional narrative structure, and the validity of its ending.

Plot

In Depression-era Oklahoma, Tom Joad hitchhikes home after being paroled from the state penitentiary. Along the road, he encounters Jim Casy, a preacher Tom remembers from childhood. Casy explains that he is no longer a preacher, having lost his calling. He still believes in the Holy Spirit, but not necessarily the spirituality mandated by organized religion. For Casy, the Holy Spirit is love. Not just the love of God or Jesus, but the love of all humans. He maintains that all people are holy, everyone being part of the whole soul of humankind. When they arrive at what was once the Joad farm, Tom and Casy find it abandoned. Muley Graves, a Joad neighbor, approaches and tells Tom that his family has been tractored off their land by the bank. They have moved in with his Uncle John and are preparing to leave for California to find work. Tom and Casy spend the night near the deserted farm and head to Uncle John's early the next morning. The family is preparing for their journey to California when Tom and Casy arrive. Casy asks whether he can journey west with the Joads. The Joads agree to take him along. Once their belongings have been sold, everyone except Grampa is anxious to get started. The family stops that first evening next to a migrant couple whose car has broken down. The Wilsons are gracious, offering their tent to Grampa who has a stroke and dies. Tom and Al fix the Wilson's car, and the two families decide to travel together. In New Mexico, the Wilson's touring car breaks down again, and the families are forced to stop. Granma has become increasingly ill since Grampa's death, and Tom suggests the others take the truck and continue on. Ma refuses to go, insisting that the family stay together. As they reach the desert bordering California, Sairy Wilson becomes so ill that she is unable to continue. The Joads leave the Wilsons and continue across the California desert on their own. Midway across the desert, Granma dies. By dawn, the Joads have climbed out of the desert and stop the truck to gaze down upon the beautiful Bakersfield valley. The Joads stop at the first camp they come to, a dirty Hooverville of tents and makeshift shelters. The men are talking to Floyd Knowles, a young man in the camp, when a businessman accompanied by a cop offers them work. When Floyd asks for a wage offer in writing, he is accused of being a "red", and the cop attempts to arrest him. Tom trips the cop, and Casy kicks him. When the cop regains consciousness, Casy gives himself up to the law in order to divert attention away from Tom. The Joads immediately leave to avoid any further trouble. The Joads travel south to a government-run camp in Weedpatch. Here, the community governs itself, electing committees to deal with clean-up, discipline, and entertainment. The Joads are comfortable but, after a month, are still unable to find any work and realize they must move on. They are offered work picking peaches in Tulare. They are paid five cents a box, not sufficient to feed the family a day's meal. After the first day of picking, Tom wanders outside the ranch. He meets up with Jim Casy who is killed later. Without thinking, Tom begins beating Casy's killer. Tom becomes a fugitive, hidden by his family. The Joads flee the peach ranch at the first daylight. Tom hides in a nearby cave where his mother leaves him food. The family is comfortable for a time, earning enough to eat meat daily. One day, however, young Ruthie gets in a fight with another child. She threatens to call her big brother who is hiding because he has killed two men. Ma rushes to tell Tom he must leave for his own safety. Tom agrees and leaves with plans to carry on the social work that Jim Casy has begun. It rains steadily, and the water levels begin to rise. After a few days, the rain subsides. Leaving Al and the Wainwrights, the remaining Joads abandon the boxcar for higher ground. They find shelter in an old barn already occupied by a boy and his starving father. The child tells the Joads that his father has not eaten in six days and is unable to keep down solid food. Rose of Sharon offers him the breast milk no longer needed for her own child. The others leave the barn as she cradles the dying man to her breast.

＼ Suggested Movie Version

The movie was based on John Steinbeck's novel, arguably the most effective social document of the 1930s, and it was directed by a filmmaker who had done more than any other to document the Westward Movement of American settlement. John Ford was the director of *The Iron Horse* (1924), about the dream of a railroad to the West, and made many other films about the white migration into Indian lands, including his Cavalry trilogy (*Fort Apache*, *She Wore a Yellow Ribbon*, *Rio Grande*). *The Grapes of Wrath* tells the sad end of the dream. The small shareholders who staked their claims 50 years earlier are forced off their land by bankers and big landholders.

The movie finds a larger socialist lesson in this, when Tom tells Ma: "One guy with a million acres and a hundred thousand farmers starvin." Of course Tom didn't know the end of the story, about how the Okies would go to work in war industries and their children would prosper more in California than they would have in Oklahoma, and their grandchildren would star in Beach Boys songs. It is easy to forget that for many, *The Grapes of Wrath* had a happy, unwritten, fourth act.

When Steinbeck published his novel in 1939, it was acclaimed as a masterpiece and won the Pulitzer Prize. It was snatched up by Darryl F. Zanuck of 20th Century-Fox and assigned to his top director, John Ford. It expressed the nation's rage about the Depression in poetic, biblical terms, and its dialogues did a delicate little dance around words.

The movie won Oscars for Best Director and Best Actress and was nominated for five others, including Best Actor.

＼ Important Quotations

Chapter 8

I got thinkin' how we was holy when we was one thing, an' mankin' was holy when it was one thing. An' it on'y got unholy when one mis'able little fella got the bit in his teeth an' run off his own way, kickin' an' draggin' an' fightin'. Fella like that bust the holi-ness. But when they're all workin' together, not one fella for another fella, but one fella kind of harnessed to the whole shebang—that's right, that's holy.

Chapter 22

"We're Joads. We don't look up to nobody. Grampa's grampa, he fit in the Revolution. We were farm people till the debt. And then—them people. They done somepin to us. Ever' time they come seemed like they was a-whippin' me—all of us. An' in Needles, that police. He done somepin to me, made me feel mean. Made me feel ashamed. An' now I ain't ashamed. These folks is our folks—is our folks. An' that manager, he come an' set an' drank coffee, an' he says, 'Mrs. Joad' this, an' 'Mrs. Joad' that—an' 'How you gettin' on, Mrs. Joad?" She stopped and sighed. "Why, I feel like people again."

Chapter 28

Wherever they's a fight so hungry people can eat, I'll be there. Wherever they's a cop beatin' up a guy, I'll be there. If Casy knowed, why, I'll be in the way guys yell when they're mad an'—I'll be in the way kids laugh when they're hungry n' they know supper's ready. An' when our folks eat the stuff they raise an' live in the houses they build—why, I'll be there. See? God, I'm talkin' like Casy. Comes of thinkin' about him so much. Seems like I can see him sometimes.

Quoted from

http://vdisk.weibo.com/s/aE3h_NIUdxZ7v.

Clip of the Movie

The part when the family ends up in a "good" camp provided by the government.

Topics for Discussion

1. The first part of the film follows the book fairly closely. However, the second half and the ending in particular are significantly different from the book. While the book ends with the downfall and break-up of the Joad family, the film switches the order of sequences so that the family ends up in a "good" camp provided by the government, and events turn out relatively well. It's more comforting, and not as controversial as that of the book. Is it more acceptable to you?

2. The film uses visual imagery to focus on the Joads as a family unit, whereas the novel focuses on their journey as a part of the "family of man". This subtly serves to focus the film on the specific family, as opposed to the novel's focusing on man and land together. What do you think of this kind of adaptation?

Chapter 17　Miller: *The Crucible*

╲ Context

In 1692 Salem Witch Trials took place in a town Salem which is nearby Boston, MA. It is regarded as one of the darkest moments in American history. The trials were a series of hearings and prosecutions of those who were accused of witchcraft. Nineteen people were executed by hanging during the trials, and one was stoned to death. The trials started with a 9-years-old girl in Salem Village and her 11-years-old cousin beginning to scream, threw things about and have weird sounds etc. Then more girls in the village began to have similar symptoms. They were believed to be victims of witchcraft. More and more people were accused of witchcraft, partly because of their remoteness from the social mainstream.

Since then writers and artists developed their imagination on the story of these witchcraft trials. Arthur Miller, the American playwright in the 20th century, did research into the witch trials and produced *The Crucible* in 1953. In the 1950s, American senator Joseph McCarthy sparked highly controversial investigations in US against Communism. Suspected communists were forced to confess and report other communists to avoid punishment. Miller refused to cooperate and suffered from being blacklisted from potential jobs. However, *The crucible* was regarded as an obvious attack on McCarthyism though the central plot of the play may have differences from the historical facts. Thus, *The Crucible* can be best presented as a deep-going presentation of how a community can be torn apart by hostility and hysteria.

╲ Plot

Salem is a Puritan New England town. While a group of girls are dancing in the forest on a summer's day, a local minister, Reverend Parris caught them. Parris's daughter, Betty, falls into a coma-like state. Rumors come that witchcraft is there in the town. So Reverend Hale, a witchcraft expert, is asked to come and help. Parris's niece, Abigail, who is ringleader of the girls, tells girls not to admit anything. John Proctor, a local farmer, Parris and rich Thomas Putnam come together and argue about money and land deeds, which shows the hostility among the community.

Hale comes and examines Betty. He suspects Abigail but Tituba, the black slave, admits to be in touch with the devil. Then Abigail and Betty join her in naming townspeople as witches. Abigail once had an affair with Proctor and still wants to continue. Proctor refuses her and Abigail, full of jealousy for his wife Elizabeth, also accuses Elizabeth of witchcraft. Proctor asks Abigail to stop cheating but she refuses. Furiously, Proctor confesses his past affairs with Abigail and accuses her of her cheating. However, when Elizabeth is asked about Proctor's disloyalty to her, she lies to defend Proctor's honor. So Judge Danforth denounces Proctor as a liar.

The witch trials grow unrest in neighboring towns. Reverend Hale asks the accused people to confess falsely to stay alive. Judge Danforth asks Elizabeth to persuade Proctor into confessing. Proctor grows angry when he is forced to confess in public. He, with others, goes to the gallows.

＼ Suggested Movie Version

As a play, *The crucible* was first performed on stage in 1953. Later, the play was adapted for film in 1957 by Belgian director Raymond Rouleau, in 1996 by English director Nicholas Hytner and in 2014 by director Yael Farber. The screenplay of 1996 film was written by Arthur Miller himself.

The film version of *The Crucible* (1996) was directed by English theatre director and film director Nicholas Hytner, who used to be the artistic director of London's National Theatre. Daniel Day-Lewis played the role of John Proctor. During the shooting of the film Daniel met Arthur Miller's daughter, Rebecca Miller, and they got married after that. Though not a commercial success, this film made Arthur Miller win the nomination for the Academy Award for Best Adapted Screenplay. And Joan Allen, with the role of Elizabeth Proctor, got the nomination for Best Supporting Actress.

＼ Important Quotations

Act II   Scene 3

Danforth: (Parris and Cheever rise.) I see light in the sky, Mister; let you counsel with your wife and may God help you turn your back on hell. (Proctor is silent, staring at Elizabeth. Danforth exits. Cheever follows, then Hathorne and Parris. Proctor and Elizabeth move together, clasp hands.)

Elizabeth: You have been chained?

Proctor: (Feeling his wrists.) Aye. The child?

Elizabeth: It grows.

Proctor: You are a… marvel, Elizabeth. They come for my life now.

Elizabeth: I know it.

Proctor: None… have yet confessed?

Elizabeth: There be many confessed.

Proctor: Rebecca…?

Elizabeth: Not Rebecca. (He smiles slightly in admiration, nodding. She then speaks.) She is one foot in heaven now. Naught may hurt her more.

Proctor: And Giles?

Elizabeth: Giles is dead.

Proctor: (He looks at her incredulously.) When were he hanged?

Elizabeth: (Quietly, factually.) He were not hanged. He would not answer ay or nay to his indictment; for if he denied the charge they'd hang him surely, and auction out his property. So he stand mute, and died Christian under the law. (He nods.)

Proctor: (Not looking at her.) Then how does he die?

Elizabeth: (Gently.) …They press him, John.

Proctor: (Looking at her.) Press?

Elizabeth: Great stones they lay upon his chest until he plead ay or nay. (With a tender smile for the old man.) They say he give them but two words. "More weight," he says. And died.

Proctor: (Nodding, smiling grimly in admiration.) More weight!

Elizabeth: Ay. It were a fearsome man, Giles Corey. (Pause.)

Proctor: (With a shy smile. Elizabeth crossing to end of bench, sits.) I have been thinking I would confess to them. (She shows nothing. He takes her hand, pulls her down to bench, not looking at her.) What would you have me do?

Elizabeth: As you will, I would have it. (Slight pause.) I want you living, John. That's sure.

Proctor: (Taking his hand away from her.) It is a pretense, Elizabeth.

Elizabeth: What is?

Proctor: (Trying to convince himself.) I cannot mount the gibbet like a saint. It is a fraud. I am not that man. (She is silent.) My honesty is broke, Elizabeth, I am no good man. Nothing's spoiled by giving them this lie that were not rotten long before.

Elizabeth: And yet you've not confessed till now. That speak goodness in you.

Proctor: (Bitterly smiling.) Spite. Spite only keeps me silent. It is hard to give a lie to dogs! (He takes her hand, holds it.) I would have your forgiveness, Elizabeth.

Elizabeth: John… it come to naught that I should forgive you. Will you forgive yourself? It is your soul, John. (He bows his head.) Only be sure of this, for I know it now: whatever you will do, it is a good man does it. (Hathorne enters.)

Hathorne: What say you, Proctor? The sun is soon up. (Proctor lifts his head.)

Elizabeth: (Warmly.) Do what you will. But let none by you judge, there be no higher judge under heaven than Proctor is! Forgive me, forgive me, John—I never knew such goodness in the world!

Proctor: I want my life.

Hathorne: You'll confess yourself?!

Proctor: I will have my lie.

Hathorne: God be praised!—It is a providence! (Hathorne rushes out door, his voice is heard calling offstage.) He will confess! Proctor will confess!

Proctor: (With a cry, rising.) Why do you cry it! It is evil, is it not? It is evil.

Elizabeth: (Weeping) I cannot judge you, John, I cannot!

Proctor: Then who will judge me? God in Heaven, what is John Proctor, what is John Proctor! (A fury is riding in him, a tantalized search.) I think it is honest, I think so: I am no saint. Let Rebecca go like a saint, for me it is fraud!

Elizabeth: I am not your judge, I cannot be...

Proctor: Would you give them such a lie? Say it. Would you ever give them this? (She can't answer.) You would not; if tongs of fire were singeing you, you would not!—it is evil. (Slight pause. Sitting.) Good then, it is evil, and I do it. (Hathorne enters with Danforth, and with them Cheever, Parris and Hale. It is a business-like, rapid entrance, as though the ice had been broken.)

Danforth: Praise to God, man, you shall be blessed in Heaven for this. (Cheever hurries to prepare to write.) Now then, let us have it. Are you ready, Mister Cheever?

Proctor: Why must it be written?

Danforth: Why, for the good instruction of the village, Mister; this we shall post upon the church door! Now, then, Mister, will you speak slowly, and directly to the point for Mister Cheever's sake? Mister Proctor, have you seen the Devil in your life? Come, man, there is light in the sky; the town waits at the scaffold, I would give out this news. Did you see the devil?

Proctor: (Looks at him, then away, and speaks.) I did.

Parris: Praise God!

Danforth: And when he come to you, what were his demand? Did he bid you to do his work upon the earth?

Proctor: He did.

Danforth: And you bound yourself to his service (Danforth turns, as Rebecca and Willard enter.) Ah, Rebecca Nurse.—Come in, come in, woman.

Rebecca: Ah, John! You are well, then, eh?

Danforth: Courage, man, courage—let her witness your good example that she may come to God herself. Now hear it, Goody Nurse! Say on, Mister Proctor—did you bind yourself to the Devil's service?

Rebecca: Why, John!

Proctor: (Face turned from Rebecca.) I did.

Danforth: Now, woman, you surely see it profit nothing to keep this conspiracy any further. Will you confess yourself with him?

Rebecca: Oh, John—God send His mercy on you!

Proctor: Take her out!

Danforth: I say will you confess yourself, Goody Nurse!

Rebecca: Why, it is lie, it is a lie; how may I damn myself? I cannot.

Danforth: Mister Proctor. When the Devil came to you did you see Rebecca Nurse in his company? Come, man, take courage—did you ever see her with the Devil?

Proctor: (Almost inaudibly, in agony.) No. (Rebecca takes a step toward him.)

Danforth: Did you ever see anyone with the devil?

Proctor: I did not.

Danforth: Proctor, you mistake me. I am not empowered to trade your life for a lie. You have most certainly seen some person with the Devil. Mister Proctor, a score of people have already testified they saw this woman with the devil…

Proctor: I speak my own sins, I cannot judge another.

Hale: Excellency, it is enough he confess himself. Let him sign it.

Parris: It is a great service, sir—it is a weighty name, it will strike the village that he confess. I beg you, let him sign it. The sun is up, Excellency!

Danforth: Come then, sign your testimony.

Proctor: You have all witnessed it—it is enough.

Danforth: You will not sign it?

Proctor: You have all witnessed it; what more is needed?

Danforth: Do you sport with me? You will sign your name or it is no confession, Mister! (Proctor signs.) Your second name, man? (Proctor signs his last name.)

Parris: Praise be to the Lord!

Danforth: (Perplexed, but politely extending his hand.) If you please, sir.

Proctor: (Dumbly, looking at paper.) No.

Danforth: Mister Proctor, I must have…

Proctor: (Putting paper behind him. Childishly befuddled.) No—no I have signed it. You have seen me. It is done! You have no need for this.

Parris: Proctor, the village must have proof that…

Proctor: Damn the village! I confess to God and God has seen my name on this! It is enough!

Danforth: No, sir, it is…

Proctor: You came to save my soul, did you not? Here—I have confessed myself, it is enough!

Danforth: You have not con…

Proctor: I have confessed myself! Is there no good penitence but it be public? God does not need my name nailed upon the church! God sees my name, God knows how black my sins are! It is enough.

Danforth: Mister Proctor…

Proctor: You will not use me! I am no Sarah Good or Tituba, I am John Proctor! You will not use me!

Danforth: I do not wish to…

Proctor: I have three children—how may I teach them to walk like men in the world and I sold my friends?

Danforth: You have not sold your friends…

Proctor: I blacken all of them when this is nailed to the church the very day they hang for silence!

Danforth: Mister Proctor, I must have good and legal proof that you…

Proctor: You are the high court, your word is good enough! Tell them I confessed myself, say Proctor broke his knees and wept like a woman, say what you will, but my name cannot…

Danforth: (With suspicion.) It is the same, is it not? If I report it or you sign to it?

Proctor: No, it is not the same! What others say and what I sign to is not the same!

Danforth: Why? Do you mean to deny this confession when you are free?

Proctor: I mean to deny nothing!

Danforth: Then explain to me, Mr. Proctor, why you will not let…

Proctor: Because it is my name! Because I cannot have another in my life. Because I am not worth the dust on the feet of them that hang! How may I live without my name? I have given you my soul. Leave me my name!

Danforth: Is that document a lie? If it is a lie I will not accept it! You will give me hour honest confession in my hand, or I cannot keep you from the rope.

Parris: Proctor, Proctor!

Hale: Man, you will hang—you cannot!

Proctor: (Crossing slowly to Elizabeth, takes her hand for a moment.) Pray God it speak some goodness for me. (They embrace. He then holds her at arm's length.) Give them no tear. Show them a heart of stone and sink them with it.

Rebecca: Let you fear nothing. There is another judgment waiting for us all.

Danforth: Whoever weeps for these weeps for corruption. Take them!

Parris: Go to him. (Drum roll off.) Goody Proctor! There is yet time! (Parris runs out as though to hold back his fate.) Proctor! Proctor! (Elizabeth crosses to window.)

Hale: Woman, plead with him! (Drum roll. Elizabeth avoids his eyes.) It is pride, it is vanity. Be his helper! —what profit him to bleed? Shall the dust praise him? Shall the worms declare his truth? Go to him, take his shame away.

Elizabeth: (Firmly, bitterly with triumph.) He have his goodness now. God forbid I take it from him. (The drum roll heightens violently. Three seconds then.)

(The curtain falls.)

Quoted from

https://www.cusd80.com/cms/lib6/AZ01001175/Centricity/Domain/ 4860/The%20 Crucible_full%20text_adobe_format.pdf.

Clip of the Movie

The part when John Proctor refuses to confess in public and goes to his gallows.

Topics for Discussion

1. How do you understand the relationship between Abigail Williams and Elizabeth Proctor?

2. What makes Judges Danforth, Hathorne and others not accept the claim that Abigail and other girls are in fraud?

3. Discuss the role of Reverand Parris, especially his motivations in pushing the witch trials.

Chapter 18　Heller: *Catch 22*

＼ Context

The famous and classic novel, *Catch 22*, was written in 1961, which was composed by Joseph Heller, the most prominent American novelist of the absurd and black humor in the postwar period. *Catch 22* is a representative novel of black humor. It does not have a complete storyline, and there are more than 40 characters in it. These characters in the absurd world seem kind of crazy.

With the popularity of the novel, the phrase "Catch 22" has become a new addition to the English language and is widely accepted by people in their daily life, which is a synonym for any insurmountable obstacles and dilemmas caused by paradoxical, illogical rules or conditions. It is well known that military regulations should be a tight organizational discipline and iron system, which have specific instructions and precise norms. What is "Catch 22"? What does it include? As a matter of fact, "Catch 22" is a non-existent existence, an omnipresent thing and an invisible force. It floats like a cloud; it changes like a dream; it has countless contents; and it works in all fields. According to "Catch 22", only insanity can be avoided from flying combat mission, but he himself needs to ask. And if he asked, he was not insane and could not stop flying. So "Catch 22" is a paradox and there is no logical.

In this novel, Heller employs anti-novel narrative structure, including narration, conversation, and recollection to organize events, plots and characters, to show the absurdity and confusion of the real world he describes.

＼ Plot

The protagonist, Captain Joseph Yossarian, is a bombardier in U.S. Air Force during World War II. He, together with his fellow pilots, is forced to fly dangerous missions. He is horrified when he sees death around him. He is afraid of death. He does not want to die; therefore he attempts to escape. At the first sight, he is not a brave solider. In fact he has lost faith in God, and feels no sense of security any more.

The main antagonist, Colonel Cathcart, is crazy about being a General. In order to please his commanding officer, he continually raises the number of missions that are required to complete to return home. Every time Yossarian is close to the number that is required, Colonel Cathcart increases the number again. The number is increased from 25 to 50, and then to 75 and finally 80 times. Yossarian learns that "Catch 22" that the Army Air Corps employs is a paradox, just as Doc Daneeka explains. Any airman "would be crazy to fly more missions and sane if he didn't, but if he was sane he'd have to fly them. If he flew them he was crazy and didn't have to; but if he didn't, he was sane and had to". So he pretends to be sick and stays in hospital one time after another. Finally he escapes to Sweden.

Major Major is just promoted to Major Major and put in charge of a squadron, but he doesn't want to be bothered. So he tells the solider that if someone wants to talk to Major Major, the person has to wait in the waiting room until office hours are over, then Major wouldn't be in his office. The visitor could enter his office.

The world Yossarian lives is an irrational, disorderly, nightmarish one. And everyone seems crazy and does something absurd, such as Milo, who is obsessed with his black market schemes. What he does is to make money, even regardless of the pilots' lives; Aarfy murders a girl he raped so as not to let her spread the gossip; Nately falls in love with a prostitute; Major Danby speaks some stupid and foolish words before every bomb runs and Captain Orr keeps crashing at sea. The repeated crash landings are the practicing and planning of his escape.

Suggested Movie Version

Catch 22 (1970 film) is an American black comedy film that was adapted from Joseph Heller's 1961 novel of the same name. It was directed by Mike Nichols and written by Buck Henry. Captain John Yossarian was portrayed by Alan Arkin and Colonel Cathcart was portrayed by Martin Balsam and Major Danby by Richard Benjamin. Other characters included Bob Balaban, Buck Henry, Jack Gilford, Anthony Perkins and so on.

Two years was spent by director Mike Nichols and screenwriter Buck Henry writing a screen adaptation of *Catch 22*. The complicate plot of Heller's novel was changed and some storylines were neglected in the film so that the story was narrated, to a large extent, in an chronological order. And what's more, dialogue was employed by characters in the film so as to make the film plot more coherent. "Despite the changes in the screenplay, Heller approved of the film," according to a commentary by Nichols and Steven Soderbergh included on a DVD release. According to Nichols, "Heller was particularly impressed with a few scenes and bits of dialogue Henry created for the film, and said he wished he could have included them in the novel."

Important Quotations

Chapter 6   Hungry Joe

Like all the other officers at Group Headquarters except Major Danby, Colonel Cathcart was infused with the democratic spirit: he believed that all men were created equal, and he therefore spurned all men outside Group Headquarters with equal fervor. Nevertheless, he believed in his men. As he told them frequently in the briefing room, he believed they were at least ten missions better than any other outfit and felt that any who did not share this confidence he had placed in them could get the hell out. The only way they could get the hell out, though, as Yossarian learned when he flew to visit ex-P.F.C. Wintergreen, was by flying the extra ten missions.

'I still don't get it,' Yossarian protested. 'Is Doc Daneeka right or isn't he?' 'How many did he say?'

'Forty.'

'Daneeka was telling the truth,' ex-P.F.C. Wintergreen admitted. 'Forty missions is all you have to fly as far as Twenty-seventh Air Force Headquarters is concerned.' Yossarian was jubilant. 'Then I can go home, right? I've got forty-eight.'

'No, you can't go home,' ex-P.F.C. Wintergreen corrected him. 'Are you crazy or something?'

'Why not?'

'Catch-22.'

'Catch-22?' Yossarian was stunned. 'What the hell has Catch-22 got to do with it?'

'Catch-22,' Doc Daneeka answered patiently, when Hungry Joe had flown Yossarian back to Pianosa, 'says you've always got to do what your commanding officer tells you to.'

'But Twenty-seventh Air Force says I can go home with forty missions.'

'But they don't say you have to go home. And regulations do say you have to obey every order. That's the catch. Even if the colonel were disobeying a Twenty-seventh Air Force order by making you fly more missions, you'd still have to fly them, or you'd be guilty of disobeying an order of his. And then Twenty-seventh Air Force Headquarters would really jump on you.' Yossarian slumped with disappointment. 'Then I really have to fly the fifty missions, don't I?' he grieved.

'The fifty-five,' Doc Daneeka corrected him.

'What fifty-five?'

'The fifty-five missions the colonel now wants all of you to fly.' Hungry Joe heaved a huge sigh of relief when he heard Doc Daneeka and broke into a grin. Yossarian grabbed Hungry Joe by the neck and made him fly them both right back to ex-P.F.C. Wintergreen.

'What would they do to me,' he asked in confidential tones, 'if I refused to fly them?'

'We'd probably shoot you,' ex-P.F.C. Wintergreen replied.

'We?' Yossarian cried in surprise. 'What do you mean, we? Since when are you on their side?'

'If you're going to be shot, whose side do you expect me to be on?' ex-P.F.C. Wintergreen retorted.

Yossarian winced. Colonel Cathcart had raised him again.

Chapter 9   Major Major Major

'From now on,' he said, 'I don't want anyone to come in to see me while I'm here. Is that clear?'

'Yes, sir,' said Sergeant Towser. 'Does that include me?'

'Yes.'

'I see. Will that be all?'

'Yes.'

'What shall I say to the people who do come to see you while you're here?' 'Tell them I'm in and ask them to wait.'

'Yes, sir. For how long?'

'Until I've left.'

'And then what shall I do with them?'

'I don't care.'

'May I send them in to see you after you've left?'

'Yes.'

'But you won't be here then, will you?'

'No.'

'Yes, sir. Will that be all?'

'Yes.'

'Yes, sir.'

'From now on,' Major Major said to the middle-aged enlisted man who took care of his trailer, 'I don't want you to come here while I'm here to ask me if there's anything you can do for me. Is that clear?'

'Yes, sir,' said the orderly. 'When should I come here to find out if there's anything you want me to do for you?'

'When I'm not here.'

'Yes, sir. And what should I do?'

'Whatever I tell you to.'

'But you won't be here to tell me. Will you?'

'No.'

'Then what should I do?'

'Whatever has to be done.'

'Yes, sir.'

'That will be all,' said Major Major.

'Yes, sir,' said the orderly. 'Will that be all?'

'No,' said Major Major. 'Don't come in to clean, either. Don't come in for anything unless you're sure I'm not here.'

'Yes, sir. But how can I always be sure?'

'If you're not sure, just assume that I am here and go away until you are sure. Is that clear?'

'Yes, sir.'

'I'm sorry to have to talk to you in this way, but I have to. Goodbye.' 'Goodbye, sir.'

'And thank you. For everything.'

'Yes, sir.'

'From now on,' Major Major said to Milo Minderbinder, 'I'm not going to come to the mess hall any more. I'll have all my meals brought to me in my trailer.'

Quoted from

http://vdisk.weibo.com/s/d0Vau97iLEKCs.

Clip of the Movie

The part when Yossarian tries to stop flying and the conversation between Major Major and the solider.

Topics for Discussion

1. As a war novel, *Catch 22* pays very little attention to the Germans, and this is surprising. Discuss Heller's intention to do so. Who do you think the real enemies are, for instance?

2. What do you think of the so-called "Catch 22"? What is the real purpose of the army regulations?

3. If you were one of the pilots, what would you plan to escape?

ChaPter 19　Styron: *Sophie's Choice*

Context

Sophie's Choice was first published in 1979 by William Styron. And in 1980, it won the first US National Book Award, which was the basis of the successful film of the same name in 1982. The protagonist of the novel, Sophie, was a beautiful, kind, versatile Polish woman. Before the war, Sophie lived a free and happy life. Her father was a professor of law, but with the coming of the war, everything had changed. Ever since the German army moved into Kraków, her hometown, disasters had followed one after another. Her father and her husband were killed and then she was incarcerated in German Nazi concentration camp. In Sophie's life, there are at least three choices, involving survival and destruction. For the first time, in order to protect her family and children, she refused to participate in the activities of the underground resistance organization. The second choice was that a Nazi officer forced her to choose one of her two children. Under such circumstance, she could not choose, but she had to choose. She finally chose her son Jan and her daughter Eva was taken away. The last time she chose not to live in the south farm with Stingo together but went back to Nathan who was a paranoid schizophrenic. In fact, the last choice Sophie made was to choose death and destruction with Nathan together.

Sophie's personal fate reflects the fate of the times. Sophie had a deep secret in her heart, and the past that could not be said to others was the root of her pain today. Although Sophie survived, she had to suffer the torment of her conscience. Maybe only death could end her pain. For her, death was a kind of escape or consolation. Death was the last redemption. The whole novel is full of sense of oppression and reflects the pain that the war causes, the collapse of people's beliefs, the cruelty of living and the search for the soul of human beings.

Plot

It is 1947, two years after the war. Stingo, the narrator, moves to Brooklyn, New York from the south. He saves enough money and longs to be a professional writer. In the boarding house that he rents, he comes to know Sophie and Nathan and becomes friends with them. Sophie is a beautiful polish woman and Nathan is her emotionally unstable lover, because he sufferes from paranoid schizophrenic at the age of 10. Sophie's beauty and tenderness make Stingo fall in love with her, and Nathan's mysterious and artist talent makes him adore. Sophie and Nathan also deeply love this writer with dreams and sincerity. Narration interposed is employed in the film to tell Sophie's history bit by bit, by Sophie talking her painful memories during World War II to Stingo, including her father and her husband being killed by the Nazis, she herself being arrested and sent to Auschwitz concentration camp where she loses two children. The most painful memory is she has to choose one from her two children. Her choice lets her daughter be taken away and sent into the incinerator. This is her secret in her deep heart that can not say to others and her painful roots.

The warmest scene in the movie is Nathan buys Emily Dickinson's poems that Sophie likes most, and they sit in bed together, and he reads this poem *Ample Make This Bed* for her:

Ample make this bed.

Make this bed with awe;

In it wait till judgment break

Excellent and fair.

Be its mattress straight,

Be its pillow round;

Let no sunrise' yellow noise

Interrupt this ground. At that time, Nathan is gentle and considerate, sitting side by side with Sophie at night. They read the poem, a poem about death, and when they read it, they have love, hope, and a desire to survive. At the end of the film, Sophie and Nathan commit suicide by taking cyanide. Stingo recites the poem "Ample Make This Bed" written by Emily Dickinson once again. They at last choose death.

❧ Suggested Movie Version

Sophie's Choice (1982 film) is an American drama film directed by Alan J. Pakula and written by Alan J. Pakula and William Styron. The title character, Sophie, was portrayed by Meryl Streep, who won the 55th Academy Award for Best Actress. And Nathan, Sophie's boyfriend, was portrayed by Kevin Kline. It is also his feature film debut. And the young writer, Stingo was portrayed by Peter MacNicol.

❧ Important Quotations

Chapter 15

The doctor was a little unsteady on his feet. He leaned over for a moment to an enlisted underling with a clipboard and murmured something, meanwhile absorbedly picking his nose. Eva, pressing heavily against Sophie's leg, began to cry. "So you believe in Christ the Redeemer?" the doctor said in a thick-tongued but oddly abstract voice, like that of a lecturer examining the delicately shaded facet of a proposition in logic. Then he said something which for an instant was totally mystifying: "Did He not say, 'Suffer the little children to come unto Me'?" He turned back to her, moving with the twitchy methodicalness of a drunk.

Sophie, with an inanity poised on her tongue and choked with fear, was about to attempt a reply when the doctor said, "You may keep one of your children."

"Bitte?" said Sophie.

"You may keep one of your children," he repeated. "The other one will have to go. Which one will you keep?"

"You mean, I have to choose?"

"You're a Polack, not a Yid. That gives you a privilege—a choice."

Her thought processes dwindled, ceased. Then she felt her legs crumple. "I can't choose! I can't choose!" She began to scream. Oh, how she recalled her own screams! Tormented angels never screeched so loudly above hell's pandemonium. "Ich kann nicht wahlen!" she screamed.

The doctor was aware of unwanted attention. "Shut up!" he ordered. "Hurry now and choose. Choose, goddamnit, or I'll send them both over there. Quick!"

She could not believe any of this. She could not believe that she was now kneeling on the hurtful, abrading concrete, drawing her children toward her so smotheringly tight that she felt that their flesh might be engrafted to hers even through layers of clothes. Her disbelief was total, deranged. It was disbelief reflected in the eyes of the gaunt, waxy skinned young Rottenführer, the doctor's aide, to whom she inexplicably found herself looking upward in supplication. He appeared stunned, and he returned her gaze with a wide-eyed baffled expression, as if to say: I can't understand this either.

"Don't make me choose," she heard herself plead in a whisper, "I can't choose."

"Send them both over there, then," the doctor said to the aide, "nach links." "Mama!" She heard Eva's thin but soaring cry at the instant that she thrust the child away from her and rose from the concrete with a clumsy stumbling motion. "Take the baby" she called out. "Take my little girl!"

At this point the aide—with a careful gentleness that Sophie would try without success to forget—tugged at Eva's hand and led her away into the waiting legion of the damned. She would forever retain a dim impression that the child had continued to look back, beseeching. But because she was now almost completely blinded by salty, thick, copious tears she was spared whatever expression Eva wore, and she was always grateful for that. For in the bleakest honesty of her heart she knew that she would never have been able to tolerate it, driven nearly mad as she was by her last glimpse of that vanishing small form.

"She still had her mis—and her flute," Sophie said as she finished talking to me. "All these years I have never been able to bear those words. Or bear to speak them, in any language."

Quoted from

Clip of the Movie

The part when Sophie has to make a choice between her two children.

Topics for Discussion

1. When Sophie had to make a choice between her son and her daughter, she chose her son. Why did she do so? Suppose you were Sophie, what would be your choice?

2. At the end of the film, Sophie chose to commit suicide. What made her do so? Besides death, did she have other choices? If she agreed to go to south and live with Stingo on the farm, could you accept it? Why or why not?

3. The film expresses the author Styron's personal views regarding the Holocaust. What are your points of view about the war and the Holocaust?

Chapter 20　Mccarthy: *The Road*

＼Context

Considered as a "cruel poetics", *The Road* was American author Cormac McCarthy's 10th work, which was published in September 2006. Since publishing, the novel has been praised and won the Pulitzer Prize in 2007.

Ten years after the nuclear bomb broke out, everything was destroyed and the earth was almost in ruins, dark, dim and desolate. Animals and plants were on the verge of extinction. Only a small number of people survived. In this desolate and desperate situation, a father and his son walked alone through ravaged America, dreaming of warm coast in the U.S. as the grey, cold climate vanished behind them. On the way, they had to overcome all kinds of difficulties, such as hunger, coldness and survival. They also witnessed the tragedy of human beings and the collapse of human nature. Often they had to make a choice between survival and humanity. This seemed a road without end, facing the evil of human nature and unknown future. What they could do was caring for each other and longing for survival.

The Road becomes a fable of the post-9/11 era. It expresses the writer's concern for the human world. The novel is a moving story, which boldly imagines a future with no hope remained. But the father and his son love and care about each other. In the face of ultimate devastation and destructiveness, tenacity, tenderness, love and care keep people survive and alive.

＼Plot

The clock stopps at 1:17. There is a long and strong light flashed, followed by a series of earthquakes. Each day is greyer than before, no animals have survived and all the crops have withered. It is cold and growing colder. And the world is slowly dying. Soon all the trees in the world will fall, and the roads will be filled with refugee vehicles and gangs carrying weapons, looking for fuel and food. The infrastructure of civilization has disappeared.

A man and his son struggle to survive after the cataclysm and walk south to the coast, hoping that it is better and warmer. On the road, coldness, food and shoes are the things they have been worrying about. Avoiding roaming gangs is the thing they have been doing. They just have a gun and two bullets to protect themselves. The most dangerous thing is that they come across a gang of cannibals and shoot one of them. And when they enter a big house to look for something to eat, they discover a locked basement, where some people are imprisoned as food for cannibals. There the man and his son almost become the food of cannibals. Luckily they get escaped. The happiest thing is that they discover an underground shelter full of canned food and supplies. They feast and bathe. They meet an old man and the boy persuades his father to share food with him. They finally arrive at the sea, but the sea is not the same as it is on the map—it is not blue. When the boy falls asleep, their food is stolen. In order to survive, his father manages to take everything back. Every day is a lie, and the father is feeling he is slowly dying, which is not a lie. And he is trying to prepare for the day he is gone. The father is shot in the leg with an arrow, when they pass through a ruined town. So his condition becomes worse and worse and eventually he dies. The boy finally finds a very good and kind family, a man and his wife with two children and a dog. And they will keep going south.

The whole film has a strong sense of despair. But people with fire in their heart still fill with love and stick to the bottom line of human nature in despair.

Suggested Movie Version

The Road (2009 film) is an American post-apocalyptic drama film which was directed by John Hillcoat. The film, which was adapted from American author Cormac McCarthy's novel of the same name, was written by Joe Penhall. Strangely, in the film, only the Old Man was given a name, Ely. The father and the son in the film were portrayed by Viggo Mortensen and Kodi Smit-McPhee respectively, the man's wife by Charlize Theron.

The film was planned to be released in November 2008 at first. But it was pushed back 4 times because of all kinds of reasons and it was eventually shown in November 2009.

Important Quotations

The boy thought he smelled wet ash on the wind. He went up the road and come dragging back a piece of plywood from the roadside trash and he drove sticks into the ground with a rock and made of the plywood a rickety lean to but in the end it didn't rain. He left the flare pistol and took the revolver with him and he scoured the countryside for anything to eat but he came back empty handed. The man took his hand, wheezing. You need to go on, he said. I can't go with you. You need to keep going. You don't know what might be down the road. We were always lucky. You'll be lucky again. You'll see. Just go. It's all right.

I can't.

It's all right. This has been a long time coming. Now it's here. Keep going south. Do everything the way we did it.

You're going to be okay, Papa. You have to.

No I'm not. Keep the gun with you at all times. You need to find the good guys but you can't take any chances. No chances. Do you hear?

I want to be with you.

You can't.

Please.

You can't. You have to carry the fire.

I don't know how to.

Yes you do.

Is it real? The fire?

Yes it is.

Where is it? I don't know where it is.

Yes you do. It's inside you. It was always there. I can see it.

Just take me with you. Please.

I can't.

Please, Papa.

I can't. I can't hold my son dead in my arms. I thought I could but I can't.

You said you wouldn't ever leave me.

I know. I'm sorry. You have my whole heart. You always did. You're the best guy. You always were. If I'm not here you can still talk to me. You can talk to me and I'll talk to you. You'll see.

Will I hear you?

Yes. You will. You have to make it like talk that you imagine. And you'll hear me. You have to practice. Just don't give up. Okay?

Okay.

Okay.

I'm really scared Papa.

I know. But you'll be okay. You're going to be lucky. I know you are. I've got to stop talking. I'm going to start coughing again.

It's okay, Papa. You don't have to talk. It's okay.

He went down the road as far as he dared and then he came back. His father was asleep. He sat with him under the plywood and watched him. He closed his eyes and talked to him and he kept his eyes closed and listened. Then he tried again.

He woke in the darkness, coughing softly. He lay listening. The boy sat by the fire wrapped in a blanket watching him. Drip of water. A fading light. Old dreams encroached upon the waking world. The dripping was in the cave. The light was a candle which the boy bore in a ring stick of beaten copper. The wax spattered on the stones. Tracks of unknown creatures in the mortified loess. In that cold corridor they had reached the point of no return which was measured from the first solely by the light they carried with them.

Do you remember that little boy, Papa?

Yes. I remember him.

Do you think that he's all right that little boy?

Oh yes. I think he's all right.

Do you think he was lost?

No. I don't think he was lost.

I'm scared that he was lost.

I think he's all right.

But who will find him if he's lost? Who will find the little boy?

Goodness will find the little boy. It always has. It will again.

He slept close to his father that night and held him but when he woke in the morning his father was cold and stiff. He sat there a long time weeping and then he got up and walked out through the woods to the road. When he came back he knelt beside his father and held his cold hand and said his name over and over again.

He stayed three days and then he walked out to the road and he looked down the road and he looked back the way they had come. Someone was coming. He started to turn and go back into the woods but he didn't. He just stood in the road and waited, the pistol in his hand. He'd piled all the blankets on his father and he was cold and he was hungry. The man that hove into view and stood there looking at him was dressed in a gray and yellow ski parka. He carried a shotgun upside down over his shoulder on a braided leather lanyard and he wore a nylon bandolier filled with shells for the gun. A veteran of old skirmishes, bearded, scarred across his cheek and the bone stove and the one eye wandering. When he spoke his mouth worked imperfectly, and when he smiled.

Where's the man you were with?

He died.

Was that your father?

Yes. He was my papa.

I'm sorry.

I don't know what to do.

I think you should come with me.

Are you one of the good guys?

The man pulled back the hood from his face. His hair was long and matted. He looked at the sky. As if there were anything there to be seen. He looked at the boy. Yeah, he said. I'm one of the good guys. Why don't you put the pistol away?

I'm not supposed to let anyone take the pistol. No matter what.

I don't want your pistol. I just don't want you pointing it at me.

Okay.

Where's your stuff?

We don't have much stuff.

Have you got a sleeping bag?

No.

What have you got? Some blankets?

My papa's wrapped in them.

Show me.

The boy didn't move. The man watched him. He squatted on one knee and swung the shotgun up from under his arm and stood it in the road and leaned on the fore-stock. The shotgun shells in the loops of the bandolier were hand loaded and the ends sealed with candle wax. He smelled of wood smoke. Look, he said. You got two choices here. There was some discussion about whether to even come after you at all. You can stay here with your papa and die or you can go with me. If you stay you need to keep out of the road. I don't know how you made it this far. But you should go with me. You'll be all right.

How do I know you're one of the good guys?

You don't. You'll have to take a shot.

Are you carrying the fire?

Am I what?

Carrying the fire.

You're kind of wore out, aren't you?

No.

Just a little.

Yeah.

That's okay.

So are you?

What, carrying the fire?

Yes.

Yeah. We are.

Do you have any kids?

We do.

Do you have a little boy?

We have a little boy and we have a little girl.

How old is he?

He's about your age. Maybe a little older.

And you didn't eat them.

No.

You don't eat people.

No. We don't eat people.

And I can go with you?

Yes. You can.

Okay then.

Okay.

They went into the woods and the man squatted and looked at the gray and wasted figure under the tilted sheet of plywood. Are these all the blankets you have?

Yes.

Is that your suitcase?

Yes.

He stood. He looked at the boy. Why don't you go back out to the road and wait for me. I'll bring the blankets and everything.

What about my papa?

What about him.

We can't just leave him here.

Yes we can.

I don't want people to see him.

There's no one to see him.

Can I cover him with leaves?

The wind will blow them away.

Could we cover him with one of the blankets?

Yes. I'll do it. Go on now.

Okay.

He waited in the road and when the man came out of the woods he was carrying the suitcase and he had the blankets over his shoulder. He sorted through them and handed one to the boy. Here, he said. Wrap this around you. You're cold. The boy tried to hand him the pistol but he wouldn't take it. You hold onto that, he said.

Okay.

Do you know how to shoot it?

Yes.

Okay.

What about my papa?

There's nothing else to be done.

I think I want to say goodbye to him.

Will you be all right?

Yes.

Go ahead. I'll wait for you.

He walked back into the woods and knelt beside his father. He was wrapped in a blanket as the man had promised and the boy didn't uncover him but he sat beside him and he was crying and he couldn't stop. He cried for a long time. I'll talk to you every day, he whispered. And I won't forget. No matter what. Then he rose and turned and walked back out to the road.

The woman when she saw him put her arms around him and held him. Oh, she said, I am so glad to see you. She would talk to him sometimes about God. He tried to talk to God but the best thing was to talk to his father and he did talk to him and he didn't forget. The woman said that was all right. She said that the breath of God was his breath yet though it passes from man to man through all of time.

Quoted from

https://max.book118.com/html/2015/1210/31191767.shtm.

Clip of the Movie

The part when the father dies and the boy meets another family.

Topics for Discussion

1. In the film, the father says his son is his whole world and protecting him is his job. So what do you think of the love of a father?

2. If the world were to be destroyed some day, would you choose to embrace death or manage to survive. Why?

3. After seeing the scene in the film, what is your feeling? In order to protect the world we live in, what should we do?

图书在版编目(CIP)数据

电影中的英美文学名著：英文 / 方凡，寿似琛主编. —
杭州：浙江大学出版社，2018.9
ISBN 978-7-308-18455-7

Ⅰ. ①电… Ⅱ. ①方… ②寿… Ⅲ. ①英语－阅读教
学－高等学校－教材②英国文学－文学欣赏③文学欣赏－
美国 Ⅳ. ①H319.4：I

中国版本图书馆CIP数据核字(2018)第171986号

电影中的英美文学名著

方　凡　寿似琛　主编

责任编辑	李　晨
责任校对	郑成业　杨利军
封面设计	续设计
出版发行	浙江大学出版社
	（杭州市天目山路148号　　邮政编码　310007）
	（网址：http://www.zjupress.com）
排　　版	杭州林智广告有限公司
印　　刷	嘉兴华源印刷厂
开　　本	787mm×1092mm　1/16
印　　张	7.75
字　　数	230千
版 印 次	2018年9月第1版　2018年9月第1次印刷
书　　号	ISBN 978-7-308-18455-7
定　　价	27.00元